How to Retire Happy

The 12 most important decisions you must make before you retire

Third Edition
Fully Revised and Updated

Stan Hinden

New York   Chicago   San Francisco   Lisbon
London   Madrid   Mexico City   Milan   New Delhi
San Juan   Seoul   Singapore   Sydney   Toronto

The McGraw·Hill Companies

1 2 3 4 5 6 7 8 9 0   DOC/DOC   0 1 0 9

ISBN: 978-0-07-170247-8
MHID: 0-07-170247-4

This publication is designed to provide accurate and authoritative information in regard to the subject matter covered. It is sold with the understanding that neither the author nor the publisher is engaged in rendering legal, accounting, or other professional service. If legal advice or other expert assistance is required, the services of a competent professional person should be sought.

> —*From a Declaration of Principles jointly adopted*
> *by a Committee of the American Bar*
> *Association and a Committee of Publishers*

McGraw-Hill books are available at special quantity discounts to use as premiums and sales promotions, or for use in corporate training programs. To contact a representative please visit the Contact Us pages at www.mhprofessional.com.

How to Retire Happy

For Sara,
who made the journey with me.

Contents

Foreword

Congratulations! You are about to read a wonderful, sensible, and simple book that will be a priceless asset to you. If you're thinking about retiring, or have decided to retire within the next several years, or have decided not to retire just yet—or even if you retired some years ago—Stan Hinden's book will help you analyze the 12 vital decisions you must make at retirement as well as offer expert advice in each area—and do so in words that are easy to read, bereft of financial jargon and gobbledygook.

I happen to be in the category "not ready to retire." While I'm chronologically 80 years of age, measured by the age of the heart that was transplanted into my chest more than 13 years ago, I'm a mere child of 38. I love my work too much to stop just yet. But I've already personally considered many of the decisions Stan discusses and will be that much better prepared when (and if!) I finally decide to retire.

Most of my own expertise, such as it may be, is in the world of finance. My entire half-century-plus career has been in the mutual fund industry, and I fully endorse just about every one of Stan Hinden's recommendations about investing for, and in, retirement. To afford a comfortable retirement, for example, does depend on the power of time and is greatly facilitated by using tax-efficient mutual funds, a breed that remains all too rare today.

Social Security is a critical part of retirement income for most families. Although we can't control the schedule of benefits, we can control the time when our payments begin, and the advice this book gives is good: the longer you wait (up to age 70), the larger the check you'll receive. While Social Security is designed to provide a minimal standard for retirement income, its stream of benefits can be estimated to have a capital value of some $300,000 at age 70. That value is even better than it looks, for it is the equivalent of a fixed-income investment, with a built-in hedge against inflation—two priceless assets when you retire.

Stan Hinden's book is also right on the mark in its chapters about making decisions on company pensions, 401(k) corporate thrift plans, and individual retirement accounts. His advice benefits greatly from his firsthand experience (some derived from his own investment mistakes) as he presents wisdom on investing during retirement—virtually all of which I heartily endorse. His five "Golden Rules" are, well, golden. Yet they are so simple and basic that too many investors give no attention to them and pay the consequences.

His advice on asset allocation and the need for significant holdings in bonds or annuities to produce income is also well worth heeding. That advice may have seemed too cautious in 2005, when the second edition of this book was published. But now, after the stock market crash of 2007–2009 and the steep recession in our economy, it seems almost prescient.

Stan recognizes that a successful retirement requires much more than a successful investment program. His chapters on health insurance, preparing for illness, deciding where you want to live, and estate planning present a whole variety of ideas, many of which I had never given much consideration. But I'm considering them now. And in his final chapter—on successful aging—he gives all of us in the sixties, seventies, and eighties age-group a marvelous compendium of good advice, including how to maintain our physical and mental energies, some tricks we can use when memory fails (yes, it happens to me, too), and how to remain actively engaged in the great game of life.

This is a great book because it fills a major gap in the investment literature. There are countless books about accumulating financial assets for retirement but few about what to do when you get there, and Stan's book offers as intelligent and comprehensive an approach as I've seen. It takes a great deal of the mystery and confusion out of retirement and, by so doing, allays much of the anxiety you may feel as the time approaches.

To say Stan Hinden is well qualified to write a book on retirement is something like saying Tiger Woods is well-qualified to hold a golf clinic. First, as the saying goes, Stan has "been there, done that." He's traded in his remarkable career as a successful journalist, retiring from his job as a financial columnist for the *Washington Post* in 1996, and has 13 years of retirement under his belt. Although he's clearly remained active and productive, obviously investing a large amount of time into writing this book ("having it both ways," as the author puts it), he knows where the challenges and opportunities lie.

With his firsthand experience in retirement, his journalist's gift for simple writing, and his considerable financial expertise, Stan Hinden has carried off with considerable success the challenge of helping those of us considering or experiencing retirement. In *How to Retire Happy: The 12 Most Important Decisions You Must Make Before You Retire*, he has done so with flair and common sense. I am confident that his wisdom will improve your own preparation for retirement and help all of us who take the opportunity this book presents to consider his helpful and constructive advice.

John C. Bogle
Valley Forge, Pennsylvania
June 3, 2009

Preface

This is the book I wish I had been able to read before I retired. If I had, my monthly Social Security check would be fatter. My company pension would be better. My retirement savings account would be significantly larger. And I'd have a better chance of making my money last during what I hope will be a long retirement.

But that's not all. If I had known what I know now, I would have been better prepared, both psychologically and emotionally, for my retirement. I also would have had a keener appreciation for the life-enhancing opportunities and experiences that retirement can bring you.

I retired from the *Washington Post* in 1996. I was then 69 years old and had spent 23 years at the *Post*—the last 12 years as a financial columnist—writing about stocks and mutual funds. All told, I spent about 45 years in journalism as a reporter, writer, and editor.

Several months after I retired, I began writing a column for the *Post* called "Retirement Journal," which chronicled my experiences as a retiree. In essence, this book is the story of my retirement: what I learned and what I think you should know about the subject. My goal is to take the mystery out of retirement and to reduce the confusion that many retirees feel.

Shortly after I left my full-time job, I realized that I was woefully unprepared to make many of the decisions that are required of a retiree. I knew little, if anything, about Social Security, Medicare, Medigap, Medicare HMOs, long-term care, mandatory IRA withdrawals, pensions, and so on. But even though I was uninformed, I had to make far-reaching personal decisions on all of those subjects. Inevitably, as you will read, I made some bad decisions and learned some costly lessons.

The job of writing a regular column about my retirement experiences opened a window for me on a part of life that I had not known much about or even thought much about. Indeed, the more I learned, the more convinced I became that preparation and knowledge are the keys to a happy retirement.

It has been said that retirement is not an event but a process. If so, that process should begin long before you turn in your retirement papers. It is simply not logical to expect that you can learn all you need to know to make major retirement decisions in a few days, or even a few weeks, as I tried to do.

So consider this book a reporter's firsthand report from the front lines of retirement. My hope is that this easy-reader tour will help future retirees better prepare for the day when they stop working full-time. I also hope the book will help current retirees find ways to improve their retirement experiences.

Retirement in America was once a casual, even a drab, "You're over the hill" experience. It was a sign that the retiree was nearing the end of his or her productive life and was even getting close to the end of life itself.

Today, retirement in America has changed dramatically. It has become an upbeat, full-speed-ahead, "Let's start a second career" experience, made possible by longer life spans, tax-deferred savings plans, and government-sponsored income and health programs.

How to Retire Happy has 12 chapters, each dealing with one of the 12 key decisions retirees must make during the retirement process.

Some of the decisions are related to our attitudes toward life and work and the complex emotions that surround retirement. We are faced with many questions: how we feel about leaving our long-time friends and colleagues at work, how we feel about relocating to a new community, and even how we feel about growing older.

Some of our other decisions involve the web of government programs and regulations that affect all retirees. They include the age at which we take our Social Security payments, the way we manage our health care, and even how we make our mandatory IRA withdrawals when we reach age 70½. You don't have to be a rocket scientist to figure out your withdrawals—although it would help.

Finally, there are the financial decisions that will determine whether you will have a comfortable or an uncomfortable retirement. I often think about that old saying, "I've been rich and I've been poor. Rich is better." Smart saving and investing can make the difference. But as the book points out, you will have to work at it.

Retirement is not a simple matter. But your retirement decisions will be a lot easier if you take the time to understand your choices. Then you can start having fun. A happy retirement is within everybody's reach. The time to start is now. The place to start is here.

Stan Hinden

Acknowledgments

My thanks go first to David Ignatius, who was the assistant managing editor/business at the *Washington Post* in 1996, when I retired from my job as a financial columnist. It was at his suggestion that I began to write a new column called "Retirement Journal," a first-person report on my experiences as a retiree. His encouragement and support were crucial to the success of the column, which led to this book. I also had wonderful support for my column from the executives, editors, and writers at the *Post*. Key to any successful journey is having a good guide to show you the sights. On my journey through the land of retirement, I have had many excellent guides.

At the Social Security Administration, for this edition, my guides included Press Officer Mark Lassiter and especially Senior Public Affairs Specialist Dorothy J. Clark, who gave freely of her time and knowledge as she helped me update the chapter on Social Security.

My guide through the jungle of estate planning was attorney Rhonda J. Macdonald. I am grateful for her infinite patience and meticulous attention to detail. I am also grateful to my friend and financial planner Jack R. May, who helped me analyze many of the investment concepts in this book. I had help finding my way through the maze called "required minimum distributions"—the money you must take out of your IRA accounts—from Christine S. Fahlund, vice president and senior financial planner, T. Rowe Price Investment Services, and Stuart Ritter, assistant vice president, T. Rowe Price Investment Services.

My guide through the complex area of health insurance was L. Sue Andersen, a principal at Andersen Benson Consulting Services in Silver Spring, Maryland. Her expertise was invaluable. My sincere thanks also go to Melissa Gannon, vice president insurance and bank ratings at TheStreet.com Ratings, Inc., for her help with Medigap statistics. At AARP, I had help from Gerry Smolka of the Public Policy Institute.

I am especially grateful for the encouragement that this edition received from Mary E. Glenn, editorial director, business, at McGraw-Hill Professional and editorial assistant Tania Loghmani at McGraw-Hill Professional.

My sons and their wives, Alan and Gina Hinden and Lawrence and Denice Rothman Hinden, and my daughter, Pamela S. Hinden, continue to hearten me with their enthusiasm for my writings and their endless patience with my efforts to find my way through an electronic world.

My wife, Sara, to whom I have been married for 56 years, not only shared my retirement experiences but provided many thoughtful ideas about the manuscript as well. Sara was also kind enough to never ask why a retired writer keeps writing.

S. H.

How to Retire Happy

DECISION 1

Am I ready to retire?

Are you ready to retire?

When the stress levels at work are unbearable, it's easy to be flippant and shout, "You bet I'm ready to retire. Let me out of here!"

At such moments, it's also easy to fantasize about all the things you could do if you didn't have to go to work every day. You can see yourself soaking up the sun on a tropical beach, whiling away the hours on a golf course, or having gobs of time to read, watch movies, or trade stocks online.

You think about all the things you've wanted to do but never had time for: cruising around the Greek islands, touring Australia and New Zealand, watching the bullfights in Spain, or enjoying Carnaval in Brazil.

And then you suddenly realize you could even buy a season ticket for your local baseball team and go to games in the middle of the week! What a luxury!

It's also quite wonderful to think about the things you could give up: all your bosses, all those memos, and all those boring meetings. Gone, too, from your life would be those rush-hour traffic jams and the frustrations of your daily commute. If your job requires you to travel, you could stop bouncing around in airplanes and trying to sleep on lumpy hotel-room pillows.

As a retired person, you'd be free to make your own schedule, to do what you want, and go where you want when you want. Ah, freedom!

But wait! Remember the old adage: if it sounds too good to be true, it probably is. Like a lot of daydreams, these visions of retirement may or may not be realistic. They may not even be what you really want when you retire.

The fact is that when you face the question "Am I ready to retire?" your answer may have little to do with your fantasies and a lot more to do with your age, your health, your family, the nature of your job, your financial situation, and your outlook on life.

So to be realistic, let's look at the pros and cons of whether you are ready to retire. We'll discuss three good reasons for retiring and three equally good reasons for not retiring.

Then we'll talk about people who have it both ways: they retire and—guess what?—they go back to work, usually part-time. As people live longer and healthier lives, the part-time option is becoming more and more popular.

We'll also look at what life is like for married couples after they retire. And we'll talk about the psychological impact of retirement—how you can go from a busy, even frantic, working life to a laid-back but productive retirement.

Three good reasons for retiring

Reason one: The time is right

If there is "a time under the sun for everything," then surely there is a time in your life when you can look in the mirror and rightfully tell yourself, "I've worked hard all my life. I've met every challenge life has thrown at me. It's time for me to stop working and to start living life my own way. These are the years that belong to me."

If this is how you truly feel, that's fine. Once you retire, you'll be free to shape your life in a manner that gives you the greatest satisfaction and happiness. But to make the most of your new freedom, you'll need a plan.

In a way, retiring is like going on a trip abroad. You wouldn't just pack a suitcase and board a plane. You'd try to prepare for your journey. You'd read guidebooks about the places you plan to visit, study currency exchange rates, and find out what kind of weather to expect. And, of course, you'd prepare an itinerary so you'd know where you were going and when.

Similarly, if you want your journey into retirement to be successful, you must do two things: First, equip yourself with the information you'll need on your journey into the world of Social Security, Medicare, Medigap, long-term care, pensions, and 401(k) plans. Second, decide what you want to do in retirement.

Doing nothing is not a viable option for most people. Studies show that people who retire from active careers and become couch potatoes often suffer from depression and other ills associated with feeling useless and unwanted.

Your retirement plan can take many forms. You can spend your time improving your golf or tennis game, coaching a kids' soccer or baseball team, working for a service club such as the Lions or Kiwanis, or volunteering for a charitable or community organization. Many retirees enjoy spending time with their children and grandchildren. I know I do.

Retirement is a great time to complete some of your long-delayed personal projects. You may want to take some college courses, learn to play a musical instrument, or try your hand at writing mystery novels or painting. Many retirees—even those starting at late ages—demonstrate unusual creativity and artistic skills.

Whatever you decide to do in retirement, your plan should have one main objective: to keep you mentally and physically active and in close contact with other people. That is the way to achieve a successful retirement.

Reason two: You've got more compelling things to do

As we age and gain experience, we often find that our goals in life become clearer. So it was with my friend Jane Hoden. Religion, faith, and community service had long been the cornerstones of her life. Inwardly, she knew that when she retired someday, she would find a way to fulfill her personal commitment to be of service to others.

"I believe God has a plan for our lives, which is revealed in time," Jane says.

"In 1999," Jane recalled, "my mother lived with us. It gave us great insight into what life is like for a person who is elderly, has significant health and financial issues, and feels that life is not within [her] control."

Jane said she soon realized that while churches focus on the needs of youth, the newly married, or active adults, they rarely address the needs of seniors. The more Jane studied the problem, the more she became convinced that forming a ministry for seniors was destined to be her calling in retirement.

In 2001, Jane, who was then 55, retired from the federal government, where she had worked for 31 years as a public information specialist and as the manager of the news division in her agency. Her government pension was reduced somewhat because she took "early retirement," but she didn't believe money would be a problem. Her husband, Paul, is a retired Air Force colonel with his own pension.

"We looked at his income and at my income in retirement, at our savings and our expenses, and we decided we could afford to retire," Jane said.

To enjoy an active retirement and pursue Jane's ministry for seniors, the couple moved to Virginia Beach, Virginia, where they became co-leaders of The Senior Adult Ministry at Spring Branch Community Church. The programs, Jane said, are designed for people 50 and older and are intended to help "retirees who need a connection to people who will provide support and caring." Jane believed that she and other volunteers would be able to brighten the lives of many seniors who were lonely and isolated.

Retiring at 55 was "a golden opportunity," Jane said.

And so it seemed until 2006, when Jane's dream was interrupted by a diagnosis of breast cancer. Three surgeries were followed by months of chemotherapy and radiation and by some deep reflection about what Jane wanted out of life. In November 2007, the Hodens left Virginia Beach for Fort Myers, Florida, where they bought an apartment at the Shell Point Retirement Community. Shell Point is a continuing care retirement community (CCRC), where Jane will have whatever assisted living or nursing care she might need in the future.

Jane, now 63, also resolved to devote more time to personal pursuits. With her health stable, she and Paul spent last summer in an RV touring the western United States. One of the highlights of her trip, she said, was meeting a real cowboy from Wyoming. She has taken up photography and is enjoying life—knowing how fragile it can be. She does not regret her desire to broaden her horizons and seek out new adventures. "Even in retirement, you go through many seasons," she observed.

Reason three: Your job is changing

My friend Larry, who is a scientist, retired from the federal government after 35 years. He was 60 when he decided to leave. He told me he was undecided about retiring that early, but organizationally, his agency was in a state of flux that he felt was not personally satisfying.

A year before he left, Larry said, potential budget cutbacks had caused major personnel reassignments in the agency; he had been moved to a position that was far afield from his specialty. In addition, old-timers were being encouraged to leave with buyouts.

So he assessed his situation and tried to figure out whether he could afford to retire. He decided he could. His government pension would be about 45 percent of his salary, and in two years he would be eligible for a small monthly Social Security benefit because he had taught college classes part-time for many years. He also would continue to earn money from teaching, and he planned to accept a three-year research fellowship that paid fairly well. "The money and research combined made it interesting," he said of the fellowship. At that point, Larry said, it seemed like a good time to leave. And he did.

"It was time for me to be unhooked from an unchallenging position and to get more involved in what really interested me, which was teaching and scientific study," Larry said.

Three good reasons for not retiring

Reason one: Work is your identity

It sounds contradictory: you can be ready to retire but not ready to give up work. What does that mean? It means that work is a habit that is hard to break. As strange as it may seem, especially on those dreadful days when everything goes wrong, work is an integral and even necessary part of our lives.

Many of us began working as teenagers and have never really stopped. In our early years, our jobs provided the money that made it possible for us to pay for the necessities of life. Later on, our work made it possible for us to pay for some of the luxuries of life. But for most of us, the meaning of work goes far beyond our paychecks. Our jobs and careers have given us our greatest challenges and our highest achievements. Our careers have helped us find our roles in society. And for better or worse, our work has become our identity.

Soon after I retired, I began having identity problems. For 23 years, I had been calling people on the telephone and saying, "This is Stan Hinden of the *Washington Post*." After I left the newspaper, when I made a phone call I was just "Stan Hinden," and I felt I had lost a piece of my identity.

This problem sometimes cropped up at social gatherings where I would meet people for the first time. At these affairs, people often look for conversational openings by asking each other, "What kind of work do you do?" In American life, it is common for people to measure the worth and value of other people by their work and titles. This tendency is unfortunate, but it happens all the time.

After I retired and people asked me what kind of work I did, I tended to stumble. I found myself saying, "Well, I'm retired. But I used to be a writer at the *Washington Post*." The phrase "used to be" didn't come easily to my lips. It was like saying, "I'm a has-been." And I didn't like that feeling one bit.

Thus, I found that not only did retirement tamper with my identity and my image of myself, but it put me in a "has-been" category that was uncomfortable for someone who had led a vigorous working life.

Reason two: You'll miss the people you work with

The idea of not having to go to your job every day may seem mighty attractive, but ask yourself this question: "Am I really ready to give up working and everything that goes with it?" That "everything" includes not only the challenges and frustrations of your job, but also the familiar, even welcome, daily routines at work.

Ask yourself also, "Will I miss the people I work with?"

These are not facetious questions. Although we like to scoff at the idea that we love our jobs, work plays an important role in our lives. It provides us with a sense of purpose and accomplishment and, of course, a place to go in the morning. For many of us, our workplace is our home away from home, the place where we spend time with a network of friends and colleagues.

That network tends to dissolve quickly when you retire and step out of the working world, as I found when I retired from the *Post* after a 45-year career as a reporter, editor, and columnist. So it's not surprising to me that many retirees say they miss work—or at least the friends and shared experiences they had at work.

This sense of loss hit me after I retired from my job as a financial writer at the *Post* and before I went back to writing part-time. It took me quite a while to figure out why—even though I loved retirement—I seemed to miss working. I was puzzled.

I knew, of course, why I liked retirement: it gave me that wonderful sense of freedom I mentioned earlier. After 45 years of working, it was delightful to be able to live by my own timetable. But why then did I miss working? Eventually, it dawned on me that what I really missed was not my work, but my *workplace*.

My office had been my second home, a place where I could chat with friends, catch up on gossip, swap office rumors, and help the other Monday morning quarterbacks decide what to do with the Washington Redskins. When I left the paper, I left all that behind. And I missed it.

Reason three: You want to stay in the loop

My friend Bert Ely is 68 years old, an age when most people are either retired or thinking about it. But Bert is not headed in that direction. A prominent Washington consultant in the field of banking and financial services, Bert has run his own business for almost 40 years. And he plans to continue to do just that.

A man of high energy, Bert says he does not ever want to retire. "While eventually I might like to trim my present 60-hour work week to 50 hours or even 40 hours and take a few longer weekends," he told me, "continuing to work full-time still seems much more attractive, invigorating, and fun than the alternatives."

Bert says he is aware that if he wants to avoid retirement, especially as he ages, he will face certain professional challenges. He focuses on those challenges by asking himself some hard questions: "How do I stay relevant in my field? What is the best way to maintain professional contacts and to interact positively with much younger peers while maintaining their respect? How do I avoid coming across as an old fogy who is trying to hang on when he should hang it up?"

A top priority, he says, is to stay in touch with the people and issues in his industry. "I'm a great believer in schmoozing, staying in the loop, knowing who the players are, being current on the gossip," he says. Staying up to date technologically is important, too. "My BlackBerry is always close at hand."

Staying relevant, Bert adds, has little to do with age and a lot to do with "not thinking old." "I suspect," he says, "that there are people out there at the age of 85 who are more relevant, more in the loop about what's going on, than some people age 50."

Retiring and working: Having it both ways

The line between work and retirement is becoming more blurred all the time. The fact is that many people who retire go back to work part-time—some even full-time. People are living longer and want to remain involved and productive.

Several of my retired friends have gone back to work part-time or full-time.

Bill Backer retired after 38 years at General Electric and then went back to work at GE under the company's Golden Opportunity program, which allowed retirees to work up to 1,000 hours a year. A marketing specialist, Bill worked about 1,000 hours a year, helping GE organize trade shows and exhibits.

Now 83, Bill worked part-time for 14 years and was enthusiastic about his "retirement" job. One main reason: "I had long-standing friendships where I had worked." These days, he said, he continues to see those friends and former GE colleagues at regular retiree luncheons.

A few years ago, Bill and his wife, Lori, sold the house in which they had lived for 42 years and moved to a nearby retirement community. The community offers a full schedule of social and intellectual activities—more than enough, Bill said, to keep him and his wife busy.

My friend Jerry Goldberg, who is 82, works full-time as a school-bus attendant in Montgomery County, Maryland. After he retired from a 30-year career in the dry cleaning business, Jerry began driving a Montgomery County school bus and did so for about a dozen years. But several years ago, Jerry suffered a mini-stroke and had to give up driving. Now, he helps handicapped children get on and off the bus and rides along with them. Jerry says he likes the health and vacation benefits that come with his job and his pay. He gets about $20 an hour and works about 35 hours a week during the school year. He said he was disappointed that he could no longer drive a bus, but he has adjusted well to his new job and plans to keep working as long as he is able to do so.

Jerry's experience is a reminder that there is an unseen factor—one's health—in all the hype about people happily working in retirement. Our ability to work depends on the state of our health. Try as we might, good health is not always in our control.

Until the 2008–2009 market crash and recession severely eroded the retirement savings of millions of Americans, it was thought that there would be an explosion of part-time retired workers when members of the baby boom generation—77 million people born between 1946 and 1964—started to retire. Indeed, the steady march into retirement began in 2008 when some of the oldest boomers took early Social Security benefits at age 62. But the "explosion" of part-time workers didn't quite happen the way it was predicted.

The retirement/part-time work picture changed dramatically after the market crash in 2008. An AARP study in May 2008 reported that 27 percent of all workers 45 and older had postponed their plans to retire. Among their reasons: losses in 401(k) plans, sharp declines in home values, and rising prices for gasoline and utilities. Note that this survey was taken *before* job losses raised the U.S. unemployment rate to 10 percent. In short, many boomers who planned to retire suddenly elected to stay on the job—and felt fortunate to have a job in the midst of a deep recession.

Inevitably, when the national economy recovers and people become more comfortable with the decision to retire, there will once again be many retirees working part-time.

Several pre-crash surveys reported that 80 to 85 percent of boomers planned to continue working—at least part-time—after retirement. While a relatively small number of people said they expected to work because they needed the money, most said they wanted to keep busy or pursue individual goals. A significant number of people indicated that they wanted to start their own businesses.

The changing nature of retirement and work was described by Neal Cutler, former director of survey research at the National Council on Aging (NCOA) in Washington, D.C. "We will see more and more people who describe themselves as retired but continue to work," Cutler said. "Many of these people are working by choice, not because they have to. In the twenty-first century, retirement will encompass a wide range of options. We will see some 75-year-olds working two jobs and some 40-year-olds lounging poolside.

"Retirement," Cutler continued, "used to be defined by what one was no longer doing—not parenting, not working, not actively involved. Increasingly it will be defined by what one does do—second career, volunteer work, travel, sports activities."

Cutler's comments accompanied the findings of a national survey taken by Harris Interactive, Inc., for NCOA and the International Longevity Center. The survey showed that most Americans no longer think you've reached old age simply because you've turned 60 or 65 or 70.

Only 14 percent of those surveyed said reaching a specific age indicates that you are old. By contrast, 41 percent said that a decline in physical ability meant you were getting old. And 32 percent said that a decline in mental ability was an indicator of old age.

As chronological age becomes less of a factor in retirement thinking, good health becomes more of a factor in keeping retirees active. Among those surveyed who responded that they were retired, 15 percent said they continued to work full-time, while 35 percent said they did volunteer work. That means that half of American retirees are not spending their time turning into couch potatoes. Unfortunately, the survey doesn't tell us what the other half are doing.

In my case, eight months after I retired I went back to work part-time, writing a column on retirement and writing freelance articles. I was fortunate. The column acted as a bridge between my full-time, 100-miles-an-hour working life and what could have been a zero-miles-an-hour retirement. Writing columns for the *Post* helped me ease into retirement gradually.

Better yet, it allowed me to stay in touch with my colleagues at the newspaper. I was happy to go to the office occasionally to pick up mail, chat with old friends, or go to lunch with business contacts. For me, it was the best of both worlds.

Retiring with your spouse: The togetherness test

When you start to weigh the pros and cons of whether to retire, take a few minutes to think about what life will be like for you after you leave your job—especially if you are married.

When my wife, Sara, and I retired from the business world, one of the questions we faced was, "What will it be like to stay at home and spend 24 hours a day with each other?"

Although we had been married for more than 40 years, we had no idea what the answer would be. In all those years, we had never been home together full-time. After our marriage, Sara spent 18 years at home raising our three children. Then she went to work at GE.

We both held busy, demanding jobs. Sara worked an early shift and I worked a late shift, so we didn't see each other on weekdays for more than a few hours. On weekends, our time was taken up with chores, family activities, or social engagements. In short, there wasn't much time to be bored. If we had a quarrel, we could go to our respective offices the next day and cool off.

Our way of life changed dramatically when Sara retired from GE and I retired from the *Post*. Gone were the established routines of office life and the constant demands of our jobs. We enjoyed a new sense of freedom, but it was accompanied by a feeling that we weren't exactly the same people any longer—that we'd lost our purpose in life.

After more than a dozen years, I can report that our concerns about full-time togetherness have faded and we've adjusted reasonably well to our new lifestyle. How were we able to do that? There were two main reasons:

1. *Sara and I did not go through the "turf battle" that causes problems for many retired couples.* A turf battle can arise when a woman, who views the home as her domain, finds that her retired husband is underfoot all day and interferes with her routine. She may feel that her territory has been invaded. He may feel that he is unwelcome in his own home—and is unable to understand why.

A glimpse of the problem can be seen in the old joke about the wife who says to her newly retired husband, "Just remember, I married you for better or for worse. But not for lunch."

Sara and I avoided a turf battle in part because she had a long career at GE. So while she did not escape the daily household chores that fall to most working women, she had not been a full-time homemaker for two decades before retirement.

In addition, we sold our house shortly before we retired and moved to an apartment. The effect was to create a new domain where neither of us had any territorial claims.

2. *Sara and I organized our lives so we had time alone and time together.* Sara retired first. By the time I retired 2½ years later, she'd already developed a schedule of social and community activities that kept her busy on Mondays, Tuesdays, and Wednesdays.

I quickly realized that Sara's schedule was an opportunity for me to get both the "space" and the time that I needed to work on my freelance writing, take care of the family finances, and exercise at the community fitness room.

So, for part of the week, we each had our own schedules. In time, with Sara's help, I began to understand the need that women have for the companionship of other women. Sara explained that her games, lunches, and shopping trips all help fill that need.

"I like to spend time with my women friends and talk about the things women are interested in," Sara told me.

Living in a retirement community, I've also observed that retired men don't make new friends with other men as easily as retired women make new friends with other women. Several men have told me that they miss their male colleagues at the office and all the chatter about football, baseball, basketball, etc.

On Thursdays, Fridays, Saturdays, and Sundays, Sara and I do things together: we might go to a new Smithsonian museum exhibition in Washington, D.C., take a day trip with friends to the eastern shore of Maryland, or just visit a shopping mall. I prefer museums to malls; Sara prefers malls. We keep the peace by taking turns.

Since we retired, we've also solved the weekly food shopping problem. We do it together. For years, Sara did almost all the food shopping, often after a long day's work. Now that I'm retired, I don't think she should lug all those grocery bags herself.

In the beginning, our shopping experiences were quite tense. We had different priorities about what to buy and different recollections of what food items were still in the cupboard or refrigerator. Apparently, we were not alone, because we'd frequently hear couples arguing in the aisles about what to buy or not to buy.

We both hated that scene. So I promised myself that when Sara picked an item off the shelf, I would stop saying, "Do we really need that?" Ever since then, our shopping excursions have become more relaxed.

On evenings when we eat at home, Sara and I get through dinner by using a team approach. She cooks and I clean up. The system has a double benefit. The meal is always excellent because of Sara's culinary skills, and that makes me happy. And Sara doesn't have to deal with the mess, which makes her happy.

This is the kind of partnership married people should strive for at all stages of their lives. But it's especially important when they're both retired.

Sara believes that if a couple wants to be happy in retirement, they need to be even more compatible than they were before they retired.

"When you retire, you'd better be friends," Sara says, "because you're going to be spending a lot of time together."

DECISION 2

Can I afford to retire?

Now that you've decided you're ready to retire—or at least decided you're ready to think about it seriously—let's talk about whether you can afford to retire.

On the face of it, the arithmetic of retirement is fairly simple. It's a matter of income versus expenses. The key question is, will your monthly income be sufficient to cover your monthly expenses?

To get started, take a sheet of paper. On one side, list all the items of monthly income that you expect to receive when you retire. Add them up. On the other side of the paper, list all your monthly expenses and add them up. Then compare the numbers to see whether you have enough income to cover your expenses.

If you do have enough income, you're off to a good start. If you don't, you have two basic choices: you can raise your income or lower your expenses. Either, as I learned from personal experience, is easier said than done.

However, there is another choice: use your savings to help close the gap between income and expenses. Using your savings is a perfectly reasonable idea. After all, that's why you saved that money in the first place. But you must plan your withdrawals carefully; you don't want to dig into your savings too often or too deeply. Your nest egg may have to help support you for 15 or 20 years. In Chapter 7, we'll discuss how you can use your savings to provide a flow of monthly income.

A change in financial situation

One of the things that surprised me about retirement was the dramatic way in which my financial situation suddenly changed. One day I was receiving a sizable paycheck. The next day, it seemed, my paychecks had stopped. Intellectually, I was aware that my paychecks would stop when I retired. But I guess I wasn't fully prepared for the emotional jolt of losing that lifelong security blanket.

In fact, there were several other major financial differences between working and retirement that I hadn't anticipated. Here are some of them.

Hello, fixed income

As full-time retirees, Sara and I are now living on a fixed income consisting mainly of our monthly Social Security benefits and our pension checks. We are fortunate to have pension checks. These days, many people do not receive pensions when they retire. But even if you get both Social Security benefits and a pension check, they are not likely to increase much over time. Most pensions are not adjusted for increases in the cost of living. Social Security usually gives its beneficiaries a modest annual cost-of-living adjustment (COLA), but for the first time since COLAs began in 1975, Social Security officials have announced that there will be no COLA in 2010 and probably not in 2011.

Goodbye, raises

When we were employed full-time, our salaries were subject to occasional improvement. We were eligible for raises and promotions, both of which boosted our incomes. We were able to work overtime, which also increased our take-home pay. And, occasionally, we received bonuses. In short, there was a reasonable chance that we could increase the amount of money we made each year. As retirees, we don't have those opportunities.

That means that the raises, overtime, and bonuses that helped pay for our new cars and summer vacations are not available in our retirement years. We'll have to find other ways to pay for large-ticket purchases or trips.

Health-care costs

Health costs are likely to increase in retirement. In fact, the non-partisan Employee Benefit Research Institute (EBRI) in Washington recently studied the likely costs of health care in retirement. This is what the researchers found:

- In 2008, a man who retired at age 65 would have needed from $64,000 to $159,000 in savings to cover health insurance premiums and out-of-pocket expenses in retirement. Even then, the man would have only a 50 percent chance of having enough money. To have a 90 percent chance of having enough money, the man would have needed between $196,000 and $331,000 in savings.

- A woman retiring at 65 in 2008 would have needed from $86,000 to $184,000 for a 50 percent chance of having enough money and from $223,000 to $390,000 for a 90 percent chance.

Since EBRI's other studies show that relatively few people have this much money in savings when they retire, the question is "Where will the money come from?" In my case, the money for our insurance premiums and other health costs has come largely from current income. I suspect that is true for many other retirees, as well.

While Sara and I were working, we both had company health insurance, which covered medical, dental, and prescription bills. When we retired, we lost our company insurance.

Fortunately, we were both over 65 and thus were eligible to receive Medicare benefits. However, had we retired at age 62—an age when many people do retire—we could have been without health insurance for several years. The alternative would have been to buy private insurance until we were old enough to go on Medicare. That insurance would have been quite costly—and would have made a rather large hole in our retirement budget.

Neither of our employers had retiree health insurance plans available for us, so we signed up for Medicare, a national program that pays hospital and medical bills for 45 million people. In 2006, Medicare also began to pay for prescription drugs. In fairness to our former employers, the *Washington Post* provides retirees with an annual cash stipend, which can be used to buy a secondary insurance policy.

General Electric, for its part, provides its retirees with a secondary insurance policy that costs $184 a month for the two of us—a relative bargain. Equally important, GE allows its retirees and their spouses to join a prescription benefit plan that provides a 90-day supply of a medication for $30.

When you begin working on your retirement budget, don't forget that you probably will have to buy a secondary insurance or Medigap policy to cover some of the expenses Medicare does not. I'll discuss Medigap policies and their cost in Chapter 8. You also may have to pay for some of your prescription drugs; payments under the Medicare Part D prescription drug program are limited.

The bottom line is that Sara and I are spending more money on our health care in retirement than we did while we were working and had company coverage—even though we paid for our company coverage.

Medicare, by the way, does not cover all hospital or medical costs. Our GE secondary insurance plan covers some of the bills that Medicare does not pay. Even so, our annual out-of-pocket expenses for health care are perhaps 50 percent higher than when we were working.

We also worry—as we get older—whether we will encounter new medical problems and thus face even higher costs in the years ahead. Medical costs can be real budget busters.

When you are thinking about how much health-care money to include in your retirement budget, you may want to consider the cost of a long-term-care policy. For a 65-year-old couple, these policies can cost about $6,000 a year, depending on the terms of the policy. For a 52-year-old couple, the cost would be about $3,500 a year. Sara and I are covered by a group policy we bought through the *Washington Post*. It costs $2,800 a year for both of us, which is relatively inexpensive, but it has limited benefits. I'll discuss long-term-care policies in Chapter 9.

The taxman cometh

In your retirement budget, you may need a special reserve for the money you owe for federal and state income taxes. During the years I worked, my employer always withheld money from my paycheck for income taxes. Usually, the amount of my withholding would be close to the actual amount of money I owed Uncle Sam at tax time. So it was easy to settle up with the IRS.

When I retired, I neglected to ask the *Post* to put tax withholding on my pension check. My Social Security check also did not have withholding. Sara and I later asked for withholding to be put on our pension checks, but we have not gotten around to putting withholding on our Social Security checks. (To do so, fill out IRS Form W-4V, Voluntary Withholding Request, and submit it to your local Social Security office.)

Initially, the effect of not having withholding on our Social Security and pension checks was that I had to file quarterly estimated income tax reports with the IRS and my state tax office. It also meant that I had to put aside a certain amount of money each month to cover the quarterly payments. I wasn't used to doing that, and it played havoc with my efforts to balance my family budget.

Here is something else you should be aware of when it comes to taxes in retirement: your Social Security payments may be taxable. Ignoring the fact that you paid taxes on the money you put into Social Security for many, many years, Uncle Sam will tax up to 85 percent of your Social Security benefits, depending on your income and your tax situation.

Indeed, it is a good idea to talk to an accountant before retiring to find out what your tax situation will be and what effect those taxes will have on the amount of money you'll have available to pay for your living expenses.

More about the taxman

As I will explain in Chapters 5 and 6, the beauty of 401(k) and IRA plans is that they permit you to save money in a tax-deferred account for many years while you are working. Such accounts can reward you by producing a sizable retirement nest egg. But when you reach the magic age of 70½ years, Uncle Sam says you have to start withdrawing money from these accounts and paying taxes on your withdrawals.

As you prepare your retirement budget, especially if you are nearing 70½, remember that every dollar you withdraw from a tax-deferred IRA will be taxable. If, for instance, your taxable income is $40,000 and you take a $10,000 IRA withdrawal, your taxable income will become $50,000, and you will be taxed accordingly. So here again, you may need to set aside money in your budget for taxes—money you'd probably like to spend on other things.

Paying for your lifestyle

As you prepare to retire, you will hear a great deal of discussion about how much of your working income you will need in retirement to maintain the same lifestyle. You will hear financial advisors and others suggest that you will need about 80 percent of your regular income when you retire. That figure seems to assume that your living expenses as a retiree will be lower than they were when you were working full-time. Well, maybe yes and maybe no.

The 80 percent rule hasn't worked for us. If anything, our living costs in retirement are higher than they were when we were both working. It makes sense if you think about it this way: When we retired, we did not relocate to a less expensive community, as did some of our friends. We stayed in the apartment that we moved into a few years before we retired. Our mortgage payments have remained about the same, but our condo fees have been rising steadily. Our food bills have gone up, too, keeping pace with the general increase in food prices. We also eat more restaurant meals than we used to—probably because we're home more and have more free time.

As for clothing, I haven't bought a new suit in some time—I don't need them much for business anymore—but there's been an increase in the amount of casual clothing that Sara and I have bought in recent years.

Moreover, early in our retirement, we continued to drive two cars because Sara and I were always going in different directions and we needed the freedom that two cars provided. After a few years, as the pace of our activities slowed, we were able to get along with one car. That decision saved us quite a bit of money on auto insurance, gasoline, and repairs.

Yes, we do save some money because we're not commuting to work every day—but not that much. We probably use the same number of gallons of gas visiting our local shopping malls.

Other expenses, such as our electric and telephone bills, have either remained the same or gone up. For instance, Sara and I both have cell phones for highway emergencies and the convenience of being able to stay in touch with family and friends. But that's $70 a month that we did not spend a couple of years ago.

Our budget also has changed when it comes to entertainment. Going out to dinner with friends is the number-one leisure-time activity in our part of the country. We also subscribe to several local theater groups and regularly attend their shows, something we didn't have time for when we were working. Tickets for those shows usually cost $40 to $50 each.

Our retirement savings, I confess, took a big hit when we began to travel after we retired. We had both worked for many, many years and felt that we were entitled to enjoy some of the pleasures that go with retirement. So we took several cruises. Our cruise to Scandinavia and Russia was memorable, but the cost of our trip was about $15,000, in part because it included a week of sightseeing in London.

My point is that when you are planning your retirement, it is foolhardy to think that you will be happy living like a pauper. You don't live that way now while you are working, and there's no reason to plan to live that way when you retire.

At the very least, make sure that your income and your expenses—adjusted for the factors I have mentioned—allow you to have the kind of lifestyle to which you have become accustomed. Remember, too, that you will want to have some fun in retirement. But the cost of fun will be extra.

If your arithmetic shows that you can keep your lifestyle and also have some fun, then you can afford to retire. But if your retirement numbers show that you can't make ends meet, even with judicious withdrawals from savings, then you may have to delay your retirement and keep working until your finances improve.

For instance, continuing to work past your full retirement age, now 66 for many people, can improve your retirement income in two ways: First, Social Security provides a bonus for every year you work past the normal retirement age up to age 70. The normal age for retirement has been moving up gradually from 65 to 66 and will rise to 67 in the future. If you are 66 in 2010 and wait until age 70 to take your Social Security benefits, you will receive four years of delayed retirement credit and a bonus of 32 percent. Thus a $1,000 monthly Social Security payment would turn into about $1,320.

Second, if you are entitled to a pension from your company and you continue to work, your pension may improve because of your additional earnings and because of pay raises. If your retirement budget looks like it could be tight, find out how much money you will receive both from Social Security and from your company pension if you work until age 70—assuming that your company will let you work until that age.

I retired at the age of 69 and found that both my Social Security and my pension were considerably higher than if I had retired at 65. Waiting to retire turned out to be a big help financially.

The power of time

When I step back and look at the list of items I have just discussed—the items that can seriously affect one's retirement budget—it is hard not to wish that I had saved more money during my working years. Indeed, I often wish that I had been wiser or more farsighted in building my retirement nest egg.

I'm not complaining. We did not save as much as some of our friends. But we saved more than other friends. So we're somewhere in the middle. And while we're reasonably secure financially, we still have to worry about whether we could run out of money during our retirement.

Perhaps if we had started saving earlier, we wouldn't have to worry about that. In recent years, I've learned that what you do about your money when you are 30, 40, or 50 will determine whether you can retire comfortably at 60, 65, or 70.

Ideally, the wise or foresighted individual will begin to save regularly at age 30, putting aside as much money as he or she can, month after month and year after year, for 30 or 35 years. Then, if the financial markets do what they have done for the last 75 or 83 years, the saver should reach retirement age with a sizable pot of money—enough to pay for a comfortable retirement, even if it lasts for 20 or 25 years. Admittedly, that optimistic scenario took quite a jolt during the 2008–2009 market crash. Millions of investors suffered 30 to 40 percent losses, or more, in their mutual fund accounts. People who were close to retirement were especially hurt. Indeed, as mentioned, many individuals postponed their retirements. People who were already retired could only look at their paper losses and hope that they had enough time to wait for the market to "come back."

In my younger years, trying to save money was a frustrating experience. As a young reporter, I was married and had three children, a small house, a big mortgage, and a salary on which I could barely make ends meet. My wife was a stay-at-home mom, so we had to manage on my modest newspaper salary. Saving money was a near impossibility.

In the 1950s, the 401(k) plan had not yet been invented, and U.S. savings bonds were the most common vehicles of the day for saving money, except perhaps for the annual Christmas Club at the local bank. In any event, I was like most young people. For me, retirement was a word with little meaning. When I turned 40 in 1967, people were "old" at 65 and were thought to be lucky if they reached the biblical goal of "three score and ten," or 70.

The concept of a long, healthy retirement that took people into their eighties and nineties had not yet emerged. It was not until the 1980s, and especially the 1990s, that saving for retirement became a national mantra, aided by the aging of the nation's 77 million baby boomers, the growth of the 401(k) plan, and the hype of the mutual fund industry.

Looking back to when I was 40, I can see why it's so hard to talk to people in their thirties and forties about retirement and to convince them to save for their futures. The first problem, of course, is that when you're that age, retirement seems just too far away to worry about. The second problem is that when you're that age, there's a good chance that your monthly bills are going to eat up every penny you bring home.

Basically, that's what happened to me. It wasn't until I was 50 or 55 years old, after my children were grown and out on their own, after my salary had improved, and after my wife returned to work, that we got a chance to do some serious saving.

While that was the good news, the bad news was that we had wasted many years that could have helped us achieve our retirement savings goals. And that was a shame, because in the battle for financial survival, the best weapon is time itself. I believe sincerely that when it comes to building your nest egg, it is almost as great a sin to waste time as it is to waste money.

Time can turn a modest amount of regular savings into a hefty amount of money. If you invest $100 a month for 15 years at a rate of 6 percent, you will wind up with $29,082. On the other hand, if you invest $100 a month at the same interest rate for 30 years, you will wind up with $100,452, more than three times as much.

The number of dollars you put into an investment is important, of course. But this example shows that the amount of time you give an investment is equally important. Why? Because money makes money.

People in the financial community often tell a story that may or may not be factual but makes an important point about saving. The story is that Albert Einstein, the eminent physicist, was once asked, "Professor, in your opinion, what is the greatest invention the world has ever known?" Einstein thought for a moment and then replied, "Compound interest!"

Now, compound interest sounds like a mysterious concept if you're not familiar with it. But it's not. Here's a simple example: Let's say you invest $100 at 6 percent interest a year and never add to it. In the first year, the $100 earns $6 in interest. You then have $106. In the second year, the $106 earns 6 percent, or $6.36, giving you a total of $112.36. In the third year, the account grows to $119.10, and so on. If you let your $100 grow and compound over 20 years, you will wind up with $321. In other words, your money will more than triple in 20 years, even though you never added another dollar to your account.

The power of compound interest can be quite awesome, especially when given enough time.

How to make your money grow

Now that we can see how money grows, the next question is "What's the best way to make your money grow in those all-important years before retirement?" There are, to be sure, many choices. But some are particularly worthwhile, because they come equipped with tax breaks that Uncle Sam hopes will encourage you to save for retirement.

Saving at work

The most important savings program, in my view, is the 401(k) plan, which many companies offer to their employees. A fuller description of 401(k) plans is in Chapter 5, but here's a brief description of the plan and why you should join if it is available where you work.

Typically, the plan allows you to contribute a percentage of your salary each week or month to a savings account set up in your name. Let's say you put in 6 percent of your pay. Your employer may then match part of your contribution by putting in, say, 3 percent of your pay, for a total contribution of 9 percent.

The company's contribution is often called "free money," but the best part of getting a "company match" is that it increases the number of dollars you have working—and compounding—for you in your account. Professor Einstein would approve.

Many companies hire mutual fund firms to manage the money that goes into their 401(k) plans. In those cases, you and your fellow employees will be given a list of the mutual funds that are available to you. It will then be your responsibility to decide which fund or funds you want to invest your money in.

When it comes to saving, the 401(k) plan has some special advantages. One main advantage is that the money you contribute is deducted from your pay before federal income taxes are withheld. That reduces your income taxes—a welcome, if temporary, tax break. Eventually, you will have to make up for those unpaid taxes—but not until you start to take money out of your account, and that could be many years in the future. Indeed, you could wait until you are age 70½.

The other advantage to tax deferral is that it helps increase the number of dollars in your account that are available to multiply and grow.

The downside of the 401(k) plan is that eventually you have to pay taxes on your withdrawals. Most people feel that's a small price to pay for the privilege of being able to build a solid nest egg over a period of many years.

One question that I am frequently asked is "We have a 401(k) plan at work, but my employer doesn't match any of my savings. Should I join the plan and contribute anyway?" I would say, "Yes." It would be better to have the matching money, of course, but you still get a tax break when you put your money into the account, and it still can grow on a tax-deferred basis.

The Roth IRA

If you are putting as much money as you are allowed to into your 401(k) plan at work and have additional money available for investment, you might want to think about opening up a Roth IRA. The Roth IRA was named for the late Senator William V. Roth of Delaware, who was chairman of the Senate Finance Committee. Unlike traditional IRAs, which give you a tax deduction when you open them, the Roth IRA does not. If you fall within certain income limits, you can invest up to $5,000 a year in a Roth IRA in 2010. If you are 50 years or older, you are allowed to invest an additional $1,000 each year.

To be eligible to contribute to a full Roth IRA in 2010, a single person must have a modified adjusted gross income below $105,000 a year. Married couples who file jointly must have an income below $167,000.

The beauty of a Roth IRA is that after you reach age 59½ and have owned the IRA for five years, you can take out the full amount without paying any taxes. Or, if you wish, you can keep the money invested without ever taking it out. Those two features can be a major advantage to a retiree.

The Roth IRA came along after I retired, so I did not have a chance to make use of it. But if it had been available when I was younger, I would have tried to fund one each year. Having Roth IRA money available would have been a major advantage after I retired.

While Sara and I were grateful for the money we saved in our 401(k) plans at work, every dollar we take out of those accounts is fully taxable. When I reached 70½, I had to start withdrawing money from those accounts, as I explain in Chapter 6.

The Roth IRA doesn't give you a tax break when you open the account. But it allows your money to grow tax free over many years. And since you can take it out tax free, that's a pretty good deal.

CONVERTING AN IRA TO A ROTH IRA

If you have been thinking about converting your traditional IRA to a Roth IRA, 2010 is a good year to do so. In 2010, there are no longer any income limits on who can do a conversion. You will still have to pay income taxes on the amount of money you withdraw from your traditional IRA to invest in your Roth IRA, but under a special rule, the tax bite can be split over two years.

THE ROTH 401(K)

The relatively new Roth 401(k) is similar to a regular 401(k) plan with one main difference. Contributions to a Roth 401(k) account are made with after-tax dollars. Thus, when money is withdrawn from a Roth 401(k), those dollars are not taxable, provided you have owned the account for more than five years and you are at least 59½ years old. There are no income limitations for contributing to a Roth 401(k) at work, but not all employers offer this new savings vehicle.

Tax-efficient funds

If, after fully funding your 401(k) plan at work and opening up a Roth IRA each year, you still have additional money available, you might consider investing in a "tax-efficient" mutual fund. These funds are aimed at reducing the amount of taxes that shareholders pay each year on distributions. The way they do that is by lowering or eliminating both the dividend income and capital gains that they would otherwise pass on to shareholders. These twin goals are achieved in several ways. First, tax-efficient funds reduce the amount of buying and selling in their portfolios, thereby minimizing capital gains. Second, they try to avoid capital gains taxes by offsetting gains with losses. Finally, they often invest in low- or no-dividend stocks that are likely to grow in market value but that do not produce income.

Tax-efficient funds are of relatively recent vintage, but they are widely available, especially from major fund companies. Index funds, which have been around for a long time, are also considered tax-efficient, because there is relatively little turnover in their portfolios. Table 2.1 shows the impact of taxes on stock fund returns.

The table presents the three-year average annual returns through June 30, 2009, for nine categories of stock mutual funds, before and after taxes. The funds are categorized by market capi-

Table 2.1 The Impact of Taxes on Stock Fund Returns

Market Cap	Value (%)		Blend (%)		Growth (%)	
Large	Pretax:	−9.88	Pretax:	−8.34	Pretax:	−6.86
	After tax:	−11.54	After tax:	−9.64	After tax:	−7.73
Medium	Pretax:	−9.42	Pretax:	−9.00	Pretax:	−8.24
	After tax:	−11.09	After tax:	−10.50	After tax:	−9.45
Small	Pretax:	−10.55	Pretax:	−10.78	Pretax:	−9.48
	After tax:	−12.26	After tax:	−12.40	After tax:	−10.78

Sources: Morningstar, Inc. and The Vanguard Group.

talization (large, medium, small) and investment style (value, blend, growth). In past editions, when past stock market returns were solidly positive, I observed that "many of the returns shown are far above historical norms and are not necessarily indicative of future returns." Given the widespread negative returns of recent years, it may be appropriate to say that the 2009 figures, too, "are not necessarily indicative of future returns."

Tax-efficient funds are likely to grow in popularity in the coming years, especially if federal and state taxes are raised to make up for the revenue lost during the 2008–2009 recession. As boomers move into higher tax brackets, they will be looking for ways to invest and reduce their taxes.

A comfortable retirement

A few years ago, I saw a sign in a Pennsylvania restaurant that said, "Too old, too soon. Too wise, too late." I have never forgotten that bit of wisdom, because it seemed to summarize my regrets about not paying closer attention to my personal finances when I was younger. It now seems perfectly obvious that I should have saved more aggressively during my working years. Social Security and pensions are helpful, but it is our savings that will make it possible for us to have a comfortable retirement. So save as much as you can. And when you finally sit down to draw up your retirement budget, your income will outweigh your expenses, and you'll be able to say, "Yes, I can afford to retire."

For more information

Books

Slesnick, Twila, and John C. Suttle, *IRAs, 401(k)s and Other Retirement Plans—Taking Your Money Out*, Berkeley CA: NOLO, 2009.

Slott, Ed, *Your Complete Retirement Planning Road Map*, New York: Ballantine Books, 2007.

Thomas, Kaye A., *GO ROTH. Your Guide to the Roth IRA, Roth 401(k) and Roth 403(b)*, Elgin IL: Fairmark Press Inc., 2008.

WEB SITES

Todorova, Aleksandra, "Understanding the Roth 401(k)," Smart Money, http://www.smartmoney.com/personal-finance/retirement/understanding-the-roth-401k-17679/.

When should I apply for Social Security?

Life is full of milestones. There are graduations and weddings, birthdays and anniversaries, and many more memorable events. Retirement is one of those milestones. I remember the day I picked up the telephone, dialed 1-800-772-1213, and told a representative of the Social Security Administration (SSA) that I was ready to apply for retirement benefits.

Several years have passed since I made that phone call, but I can clearly recall that I was nervous as I notified the U.S. government that at the age of 69, I had decided to retire. I guess I was nervous because making that call was akin to saying to myself, "OK, pal, this is it. Your retirement is official. There's no going back."

After that, it took me a while to realize how quickly the phone call to the SSA changed my status in life. One moment I was an active, hardworking member of the American workforce with a paycheck coming in regularly. The next moment, I was a retired person who would henceforth depend on Social Security benefits to help me pay for my living expenses.

I wasn't entirely comfortable with the idea of being so dependent on Social Security. But it was exhilarating to think that after 50 years of contributing to the system, I was finally going to get something back. At that point, I wasn't sure how much I would get each month, but I knew that it would be an important part of my retirement income. I was also comforted to know that the payments would continue for the rest of my life.

In fact, it was only after Sara and I decided to retire—and applied for our benefits—that we began to learn how Social Security works. Fortunately, we had not needed any of the agency's support services earlier in our lives. But that meant that we'd had no occasion to learn about the workings of its many benefit programs.

I realize now that I arrived at retirement age with little knowledge of the role Social Security plays in our national life. Nor did I understand the value of the safety net that the SSA provides for millions of elderly and disabled Americans and for families that have lost their breadwinners.

Like many Americans, I tended to think of Social Security as a savings bank. I thought that the payroll taxes taken out of my salary each payday would be deposited in Washington, earn interest, and eventually be returned to me when I retired. I could not have been more wrong, for that is not the way the system works.

Social Security, I discovered, is not a bank at all. It is, essentially, a national social insurance program that uses the taxes paid by American workers and their employers to create a giant pool of money. It's a pay-as-you-go system, in the sense that the money that goes into the pool is then paid out to people eligible for benefits. Indeed, one of the main concerns about the future of Social Security is that we will reach a time when there will be far fewer people putting money into the pool than are taking money out.

The key goal of Social Security is to provide a minimum income—sometimes called a "floor of protection"—for workers and their families. Among these individuals are people who reach retirement age, workers who become disabled, and families that lose their wage earners. An estimated 94 percent of all American workers contribute to the system.

Social Security's programs provide valuable income protection to disabled persons and surviving family members. Here are some examples: For a medium wage earner who became disabled at age 30 in 2008 with a spouse age 28 and two children (a two-year-old and a newborn), the "insurance value" of disability benefits up to age 67 was equal to a $329,000 disability policy.

At the same time, if this worker were to have died at age 30, the income protection to the survivors would have been equal to a $476,000 life insurance policy.

Clearly, Social Security is more than a retirement program, and the SSA's figures show that to be true. In 2008, almost 51 million Americans received almost $615 billion in benefits. Here's how the $615 billion were shared:

- Sixty-nine percent of the benefits went to nearly 35 million retired workers and their dependents. The average monthly benefit was $1,153.
- Eighteen percent went to more than 9 million disabled workers and their dependents. The average monthly benefit was $1,063.
- Thirteen percent went to nearly 7 million survivors of deceased workers. The average monthly payment was $1,112.

The importance of the safety net becomes even more apparent when you dig into those figures and find that

- Social Security benefits were received by 88 percent of married couples and 86 percent of nonmarried persons aged 65 and older.
- Social Security was the major source of income (providing at least 50 percent of total income) for 53 percent of aged beneficiary couples and 73 percent of aged nonmarried beneficiaries.
- Social Security provided 90 percent or more of the income of 21 percent of aged beneficiary couples and 44 percent of aged nonmarried beneficiaries.

What are your benefits based on?

When it comes time to pay benefits to retirees, how does the agency decide who gets what? It's a question I never thought about, and I doubt whether many other people have done so either. The fact is that there is a specific social philosophy that determines the payment of benefits, and this philosophy has several components. For instance, the formulas are designed so that there is a clear link between what you pay into the system during your working years and the benefits you receive when you retire. People who earn high wages during their careers generally will get higher benefits than people who earn low wages.

However, one key feature of the payment philosophy tends to level the playing field: the formula used to compute benefits includes factors that ensure that lower-paid workers get a higher return than highly paid workers. Social Security's progressive benefit structure helps compensate for the fact that low-wage earners have less opportunity to save and invest.

Low-wage earners who retired at 66 in January 2009 had about 56 percent of their preretirement income replaced by Social Security; high-wage earners had about 34 percent of their preretirement income replaced by Social Security.

This idea of paying out benefits according to the relative needs of individuals and their families carries through when the agency deals with the disabled and with families that experience the death of their primary wage earner. For instance, a disabled worker with a family to support will draw higher benefits than a disabled worker with no dependent family.

Inevitably, some people get far less in Social Security benefits than they contributed. Others get far more. A worker who contributes to Social Security for 30 years but dies before he or she can retire gets no retirement benefit. On the other hand, a widow with two young children whose husband dies at age 35 will draw benefits for many years even though her husband contributed relatively little money to the system.

Looking back, I wish I had learned about Social Security long before I retired. The agency offers future retirees several retirement options that I did not know about, each with its own advantages and disadvantages. In the end, I might have retired exactly when I did, but it would have been wise to learn about my options in advance.

As I said earlier, I retired at the age of 69. I draw a Social Security benefit of $2,123 a month thanks to a lifetime of steady work, salary increases, a blind love of the newspaper business that kept me working for four years past my normal retirement age of 65, plus Social Security's cost-of-living adjustments.

Sara, who worked for GE for 22 years, draws a Social Security benefit of $1,355. We're grateful for both payments, which are an important part of our retirement income.

But as we discovered—somewhat too late, perhaps—the time to start thinking about Social Security is when you are in your fifties or early sixties.

Your first opportunity to retire and receive Social Security benefits comes at age 62. After that, you can take benefits at any age, although most people do so by the time they are 70. The choice is yours. But there are several things you should know, because they may affect the timing of your decision.

However, before we discuss retirement options, let's take a small detour to discuss several major changes that are taking place in Social Security's retirement benefits.

Raising the retirement age

For as long as anyone can remember, age 65 was the "normal" retirement age. The SSA called age 65 the "full retirement age," meaning that at age 65 you became eligible to receive full retirement benefits.

But that rule began to change after Congress decided to raise the full retirement age from 65 to 67. The change was part of a sweeping 1983 measure that strengthened Social Security's finances.

The 1983 package not only boosted the retirement age, it also boosted payroll tax rates for workers, employers, and the self-employed, and it delayed cost-of-living adjustments and levied taxes on benefits received by some high-income beneficiaries. The SSA estimates that between 2009 and 2014 alone, the increase in the retirement age will save the federal government billions of dollars.

Table 3.1 shows the age one must reach to qualify for full Social Security benefits. The upward move from age 65 to age 67, as shown in the table, began in 2003 and affected persons born in

1938. In 2003, an individual born in 1938 who wanted to retire had to be age 65 and two months in order to qualify for full retirement benefits. After that, the age for receiving full benefits continued to climb gradually, reaching 66 in 2009 and rising to age 67 over a 22-year period. However, for 11 of those interim years, between 2009 and 2020, the retirement age will remain at 66. It will then resume its upward path, reaching 67 in 2027.

In deciding to increase the retirement age, Congress cited improvements in the health of older people and dramatic increases in life expectancy. Today, at age 65, men can expect to live until almost 82. At age 65, women can look forward to living until 84.

Although 2003 was the first year in which people had to be somewhat older than 65 to retire with full benefits, the impact of the age change was felt for the first time in 2000 by people who

Table 3.1   Full Retirement Age Goes from 65 to 66 . . . to 67

Year of Birth	Full Retirement Age
1937 or earlier	65
1938	65 and 2 months
1939	65 and 4 months
1940	65 and 6 months
1941	65 and 8 months
1942	65 and 10 months
1943–1954	66
1955	66 and 2 months
1956	66 and 4 months
1957	66 and 6 months
1958	66 and 8 months
1959	66 and 10 months
1960 and later	67

Note: Persons will still be able to take their retirement benefits at age 62, but the payments will be reduced.

Source: Social Security Administration.

retired at age 62. The following describes how they were affected and how the early-retirement option was changed.

Your retirement options

Option one: early retirement

Even though the retirement age is rising to 67, you will still be able to retire at age 62 if you are willing to take a permanently reduced Social Security payment. The idea behind the reduction is this: because you are likely to be drawing benefits for a longer period of time, you get less money per month at age 62 than if you retired at your normal retirement age.

How much is the reduction? Until 2000, if you retired at 62, you got 80 percent of your benefits, a reduction of 20 percent. However, as the retirement age rises from 65 to 67, the deduction for early retirement at 62 will increase gradually to 30 percent. For instance, if your full retirement age was 65 and two months and you retired at 62 in 2000, you got only 79.17 percent of your benefits, a reduction of 20.83 percent. If your full retirement age was 65 and four months and you retired at 62 in 2001, you got 78.33 percent of your full benefits, a reduction of 21.67 percent. The reduction will increase slowly until it reaches 30 percent for people who retire at age 62 in 2022.

Here's a retirement warning: if you are a married man who is thinking about retiring at 62, you may want to consider the impact that early retirement could have on your spouse. Here is an example.

John Q. Worker retires at 62 and takes a reduced Social Security payment of $750 a month. That figure represents a 25 percent reduction from the $1,000 a month he would have gotten if he retired at 66. His spouse, Mary Q. Worker, also retires at 62 and gets a benefit of $600 a month.

When John is 70, he dies. Mary is entitled to receive her husband's $750 monthly payment instead of her $600 payment because his is more than hers.

However, while Mary will get $750, it is far less than the $1,350 they were receiving together. If John had waited until he was 66 to retire, he would have gotten $1,000 a month. On his death, Mary also would get $1,000 a month.

Because women tend to outlive men, that's a scenario that is worth thinking about before you make your decision about when to retire.

Option two: normal retirement

You can retire at whatever age you become eligible for full retirement benefits.

One key question to consider before taking your benefits when you reach your full retirement age is "Do you want to delay retirement to increase your monthly Social Security benefit?" To answer this question, consider how the Social Security system works. Your retirement benefits are based on your earnings history and other factors. This means that you will get a specific amount of Social Security benefits over your lifetime if you live to an average age.

If you begin taking benefits early at 62, you will get more monthly payments but with fewer dollars in each check. If you don't take your benefits until you are at your normal retirement age, you will get fewer monthly checks but with more dollars in each check. In addition, those who work beyond 65 may get additional benefits because of their extra years of work.

Option three: late retirement

You can work past your full retirement, which increases your monthly benefits. For people who turned 66 in 2009, a special yearly credit of 8 percent will be added for each year they delay retirement. The bonus ends at age 70.

People who were born in either 1935 or 1936 and work until age 70 would get an annual 6 percent bonus for five years, or a total of 30 percent more than they would have gotten if they retired at 65. That bonus will rise 0.5 percent every two years in the future, reaching 8 percent for people born in 1943 and later.

The increases for delayed retirement are shown in Table 3.2. If you delay your retirement beyond your full retirement age, Social Security benefits will be increased by a certain percentage, depending on your date of birth. The increase in benefits stops when you reach age 70, even if you continue to delay taking benefits.

In 2027, when the full retirement age will be 67, people who work until age 70 will get only three years of bonus payments.

Which option is best?

After I retired, I began to wonder what is the best age at which to take your retirement benefits. Is it 62, 66, or 70?

The answer is that there is no one "best age" for everyone—even though almost half the people who apply for retirement benefits do so at age 62. There are many reasons why it might be prudent to

Table 3.2 Social Security Delayed Retirement Credits

Year of Birth	Yearly Rate of Increase (%)
1930	4.5
1931–1932	5.0
1933–1934	5.5
1935–1936	6.0
1937–1938	6.5
1939–1940	7.0
1941–1942	7.5
1943 or later	8.0

Source: Social Security Administration.

wait until 66 or even 70. Even so, the decision is a highly personal one, and before you apply for benefits, you should consider these factors: your current cash needs, your health and family longevity, your other retirement income sources, your future financial needs and obligations, and whether you plan to work in retirement.

It is important to realize that if you live to the average life expectancy for someone your age, you will receive about the same amount in lifetime benefits no matter what age you choose to start receiving benefits. Thus, the question is not how to earn the most total dollars on Social Security but how to choose the size and timing of your monthly benefit.

For example, if you take benefits at 62, you will get a reduced payment but for a longer period of time; at 66, you will get a larger payment but for a shorter period of time; at 70, you will get the largest check for the shortest time period.

I asked SSA's actuaries to give me an example of how these monthly amounts would differ. They provided a hypothetical example of an individual who retired at 62 in 2009 with career-average indexed earnings of $41, 680. If the person took his or her benefits at 62, the individual would receive about $1,132 a month. If the same person waited to take benefits at age 66, the monthly payment would be $1,510. If the person waited longer still and took benefits at 70, the payment would be $1,993 a month. Clearly, if you will need the largest payment possible when you reach 70, it might pay to wait.

The folks at SSA are quick to point out that benefit amounts for real individuals could differ significantly from these estimates, depending on the worker's actual earnings and the actual cost-of-living adjustments. Also, since SSA bases your benefit, in part, on your average earnings over a 35-year period, your monthly payment could go up if your peak earning years were to occur between ages 66 and 70. In any event, the total amount of benefits you receive will depend on how long you live.

Social Security strategies

In the last few years, researchers have begun studying ways for retirees to maximize the benefits available to them from Social Security. Their studies have focused on a little-used Social Security regulation known as "file and suspend." The provision can give retirees added flexibility when they are trying to decide on the best way to take, or delay, the Social Security benefits to which they are entitled.

The phrase "file and suspend" means that an individual who has reached full retirement age can file for Social Security benefits and then immediately suspend the payment of those benefits. Why would someone do that? Because it opens the door to several strategies that may prove financially advantageous for a retiree and spouse. (Although Social Security is gender neutral, I will discuss this question in husband-and-wife terms.)

To help clarify the "file and suspend" strategy, here is an example of how it works.

Mary Smith, the wife, is 63, and her husband, John Smith, is 62. The full retirement age for both is 66.

Mary applies for Social Security retirement benefits at her full retirement age of 66 and receives $940 a month based on her work record.

One year later, when John turns 66, he applies for his Social Security benefits, which are estimated to be $2,060 a month based on his work record.

Now that John has filed for benefits, Mary is entitled to a spousal benefit. After applying, she will receive a total of $1,030 a month (her own $940 plus an additional $90)—making her total benefit one half the benefit that John would receive at his full retirement age.

After John applies for benefits, he voluntarily suspends his benefit. Mary continues to receive the $1,030 a month, adjusted each year for the cost-of-living adjustment (COLA).

When John becomes 70 years old, he starts receiving his benefit. Because he waited to collect until age 70, he has earned delayed retirement credits at the rate of 8 percent a year—or a total increase of 32 percent—plus his COLAs. Let's say that at age 70 John's benefit is about $2,802 a month.

If John dies and Mary survives him, she would be entitled to a widow's benefit of $2,802, which includes John's delayed retirement credits. By waiting for benefits, John not only earned a higher monthly Social Security benefit for himself, but he also will have left Mary with a substantial widow's benefit.

It should be noted that the "file and suspend" strategy may be useful for some individuals but not for others. Social Security experts point out that the success of the strategy depends heavily on one's longevity. If, in our example, John suspended his benefits at 66 but died before he reached 70, he would have lost several years of payments.

Prospective retirees should therefore consider the state of their health and whether they come from long-lived families before deciding to suspend their Social Security payments. Also, the strategy may work for individuals who have enough money or investments to support them in retirement until they reach age 70. If not, they may not be in a position to suspend their benefits for several years.

According to the SSA, these are the basic rules for "file and suspend":

1. A request for voluntary suspension of retirement benefits applies only to the worker and no adjustment in benefits will be made to others receiving benefits on the worker's record, such as a spouse and/or children.

2. Voluntary suspension can be elected during the filing of an initial claim or subsequently to entitlement of benefits in writing or orally. There is no prescribed form or question on the application that is used to elect voluntary suspen-

sion. In an initial claim filed in the local Social Security office, the filer will make the request known to the interviewer and the request will be included in the remarks section of the application. If filed online, the filer can use the remarks section of the Internet application to request voluntary suspension. Additionally, if elected subsequently to entitlement, the beneficiary can make the request to Social Security in writing or orally.

3. Once the suspension is elected, it continues until the beneficiary requests resumption of payment or through the month before the attainment of age 70. In either case, payments will resume without a need to file again with an increase in benefits resulting from the delayed retirement credits.

4. Resumption of payments can be either a written or oral request. It can be requested by simply calling our toll-free number at 1-800-772-1213. We will accept a written letter by mail or an oral or written request if the requestor chooses to visit a local Social Security Office.

Who pays for Social Security benefits?

We all do. Employers and employees pay equal amounts toward Social Security and Medicare. The tax rate in 2010 is 7.65 percent for employers and the same for employees. Of that amount, 6.2 percent is used to finance Social Security retirement, disability, and survivors' benefits, and 1.45 percent goes toward the Medicare program. In 2010, employers will withhold 7.65 percent of an employee's wages, up to $106,800. Employers pay a matching amount.

If an employee earns more than $106,800, the employer continues to withhold 1.45 percent of the rest of the worker's wages for Medicare. The employer pays an equal amount.

Self-employed people pay both the employee's and employer's tax, a total of 15.3 percent. However, self-employed persons can deduct one half of that amount from their income for tax purposes.

Table 3.3   How Much of
Your Income Will Be Taxed
for Social Security?

Year	Up To
2004	$87,900
2005	$90,000
2006	$94,200
2007	$97,500
2008	$102,000
2009–2011	$106,800
2012	$114,900
2013	$119,400
2014	$124,200

Source: Social Security Administration Projections.

As shown in Table 3.3, the amount of wages that can be taxed for Social Security contributions will continue to rise above the $106,800 level each year. By 2014, the maximum wages for Social Security levies are projected to be $124,200.

How do you qualify for Social Security?

If you were born in 1929 or later, you will need 40 credits to be eligible for retirement benefits. You earn your credits during your working years. Generally speaking, 40 credits represent 10 years of employment. Here's how eligibility is determined.

During your years of employment, your wages are posted on your Social Security record, and you earn credits based on those wages. The credits are used to determine your eligibility for retirement benefits or for disability or survivor benefits if you should become disabled or die.

In 2010, you receive one credit for each $1,120 of earnings, up to a maximum of four credits per year. The SSA folks predict that, in the future, it will take even more dollars to earn a credit than it does today because of the steady national increase in average annual wages.

Note that when it comes to qualifying for retirement benefits, there are special rules for the self-employed, for people in the military, for farm and domestic workers, and for those who work for nonprofit organizations. There also are special rules for workers not covered by Social Security, as well as special guidelines for those claiming disability and survivor benefits. All this information can be found in SSA Publication 05-10072, *How You Earn Credits*. Request a copy at www.socialsecurity.gov or call 1-800-772-1213.

How much will you get?

In October 1999, the SSA began mailing annual, individualized Social Security statements to workers 25 or older who are not yet getting Social Security benefits. Statements should arrive in your mailbox each year about three months before your birth month. The statements contain a record of your earnings and estimates of your retirement and disability benefits. If you don't get a statement, request one at www.socialsecurity.gov or call 1-800-772-1213.

What will the statement tell you? Quite a lot, actually. It will give you an estimate of your benefits at age 62, at full retirement age, and at 70. The age-62 estimate will include the reduction for early retirement; the age-70 estimate will include the credits given for delayed retirement. It will also give you an estimate of the amount of monthly disability benefit you could be entitled to and an estimate of the monthly benefit that your family could receive should you die.

What is your retirement benefit based on? Basically, Social Security retirement benefits are based on the amount of money you earned during your lifetime—with an emphasis on the 35 years in which you earned the most. This information is fed into

SSA computers and subjected to several formulas we discussed earlier.

Eventually, the SSA arrives at your basic benefit, or primary insurance amount (PIA). The PIA is what the agency considers to be your full retirement amount. The annual benefits statement should be of great help to people who are eager to know how much money they can expect to receive when they retire.

Conceivably, if this annual look ahead shows some individuals that their future benefits will be small, it could inspire these low-wage earners to increase their efforts to earn higher salaries in order to improve their chances of drawing higher retirement benefits.

Applying for Social Security benefits

There are three basic ways to apply for Social Security retirement benefits. One is to apply online at www.socialsecurity.gov and click on "Applying Online for Retirement Benefits." Other ways are to call the SSA and start the application process over the telephone or to ask for an appointment at your local Social Security office and apply in person.

Social Security's toll-free telephone number, 1-800-772-1213, operates 24 hours a day, including weekends and holidays. The phone reps are available from 7 a.m to 7 p.m. on business days. People who are deaf or hard of hearing can call a toll-free "TTY" number, 1-800-325-0778.

When you call to apply for retirement benefits, the phone rep will schedule a telephone interview for you. At that time, you will be asked a number of questions, and you will be requested to mail the originals of several important documents. When the documents are received by the SSA, they will be copied and returned to you.

If you would prefer to apply in person, the phone reps will make an appointment for you to visit your local SSA office. You also can use the toll-free line to inform the agency that you have changed your address or to arrange to have your monthly payment sent directly to your bank.

The information and documents you will need when you apply for retirement benefits generally include the following:

- Your Social Security number
- Your birth certificate
- Your W-2 forms or self-employment tax return for the previous year
- Your military discharge papers if you served in the armed forces
- Your spouse's birth certificate and Social Security number if he or she is applying for benefits
- Proof of U.S. citizenship or lawful alien status if you (or a spouse who is applying for benefits) were not born in the United States
- The name of your bank and your account number so that your benefits can be deposited directly into your account

The special-payments problem

Sometimes the best way to learn about a problem is to experience it. That's what happened to my wife and me. Sara retired in 1993, two and a half years before I did. As I recall, we each phoned the SSA and later visited our local office, bringing the required documents.

Dealing with the SSA was a relatively pleasant and low-key experience—at least until we ran into Sara's "special-payments" problem. That turned into a pretty confusing and nerve-wracking situation. Here's what happened.

Sara retired from General Electric on December 31, 1993, and began receiving Social Security benefits in February 1994. When Sara had applied for benefits several months earlier, she was asked what she expected to earn in 1994. Her answer was that she didn't expect to earn anything in 1994 because she was retiring and would not be working. However, when Sara retired, GE owed her $27,231 in severance pay and vacation pay, all related to her working years. Because she retired December 31, that money was paid to Sara early in 1994 and was reported on our income taxes for 1994.

In August 1995, Sara received a letter from the SSA saying, in effect: You told us that you would not earn any money in 1994, but now we see that you reported earnings of $27,231. So, unless there are some things we don't know about, you have to give back $5,183 of your 1994 Social Security payments!

That letter sent Sara and me into overdrive, and after a flurry of phone calls and visits to our local SSA office, we finally discovered the problem: the agency did not know that the $27,231 represented severance and vacation pay that was due her for her work at GE before she retired.

That fact was important, because the SSA has a special set of rules that apply to those kinds of payments after you retire. Under these rules, Social Security does not count as earnings some types of "special payments" you receive after you leave your job—if the payments are related to services you provided to your company before you retired.

Sara was able to prove that she had not worked in 1994 by furnishing a letter from her employer, which showed that the $27,231 came from severance pay, vacation pay, and other monies owed. The SSA agreed that they were, indeed, "special payments," so Sara did not have to return any of her Social Security benefits.

While the situation was resolved to our satisfaction, it left us with a few more gray hairs than we had before. Several years later, when I retired from the *Washington Post* with my own severance and vacation pay package, I remembered Sara's experience. So I asked the newspaper to give me a letter showing what my payments covered. I filed the letter with Social Security and thus managed to head off a demand that I return a chunk of my Social Security benefits. When you retire, watch out for this one!

Running into the earnings limits

At first, Sara and I didn't understand why Social Security even cared about whether she earned any money after she retired. It took us a while to figure out that Sara had run into the Social Security "earnings limits." As it turned out, she didn't work in 1994 or earn any money in any manner, but the SSA initially assumed that she had worked and had gone over the earnings limit.

In the course of clearing up the confusion, we learned that if retirees work and go over the earnings limit, they have to give back some of their benefits. What we discovered was that, in those years, there were two types of earnings limits. One applied to people who were between ages 62 and 64. The other applied to people between 65 and 69. At 70, you were free to earn as much as you wanted.

In 2000, Congress made a significant change in the earnings limits. Here's the story.

At the start of 2000, if you were 65 to 69, you were scheduled to lose $1 in current benefits for every $3 you earned above $17,000. Thus, if you earned $20,000, you would have lost $1,000 in current benefits. At least that was the rule until April 2000, when Congress voted to repeal that part of the earnings limit, retroactive to January 1, 2000. President Clinton signed the bill April 7, 2000, with considerable fanfare.

However, the other half of the earnings limit, which affected people below full retirement age, remained intact. Since then, earnings limits have been increased steadily, although they remained the same in 2009 and 2010.

In 2010, $1 in benefits is withheld for every $2 in earnings above the limit of $14,160. A different limit applies in the year in which you reach full retirement age. For people attaining full retirement age in 2010, $1 in benefits is deducted for every $3 in earnings above the limit of $37,680—but only until the month of your birthday. All this information can be found in SSA Publication 05-10069, *How Work Affects Your Benefits*. Request a copy at www.socialsecurity.gov or call 1-800-772-1213.

Sara's run-in with those "special payments" could be experienced by anyone under full retirement age who retires and is given severance or vacation pay for service to the company while he or she was still working. In that case, get your company to give you a letter explaining the payments, and send the letter to the SSA. Meanwhile, it does not appear that the earnings limit for people under full retirement age will be repealed anytime soon.

While there was widespread support for repealing the limit on the 65-to-69 age group, similar support was lacking for repeal of the limit on the 62-to-64 age group. For instance, former SSA Commissioner Kenneth S. Apfel supported repeal for the older group in order to encourage older workers to stay in the labor force. However, he opposed repeal for the younger group because of the long-term impact on millions of elderly widows.

As I mention earlier in this chapter, people who retire at 62 whose full retirement age is 65 have their retirement benefits permanently reduced by 20 percent to account for the fact that they will be receiving payments for a longer period of time. When married men retire at 62 and take reduced benefits, it can have a serious impact on their spouses.

Eventually, when these men die, their widows receive benefits that are even further reduced. Apfel said that repealing the earnings limits for the 62-to-64 age group would encourage more people to retire younger, and that, he believed, would cause a significant increase in poverty, especially for elderly widows.

Repeal of the earnings limit

The repeal of a major portion of the Social Security earnings limit in 2000 was, as you might imagine, an occasion for many retirees to celebrate. The rule was extremely unpopular with retirees who wanted to work but did not like the idea of giving up part of their current benefits to do so. In fact, until the law's repeal, many of my fellow retirees had had a special reason to celebrate when they reached their seventieth birthdays: turning 70 meant they could work and earn as much as they wanted. Now they can do so at full retirement age, as shown in Table 3.1.

Until the law was partially repealed, about 900,000 beneficiaries between the ages of 65 and 69 gave up part or all of their current Social Security payments each year—a total of $6 billion—because they earned more than the law allowed. To avoid losing some of their Social Security payments, many retirees in America worked "up to the limit" each year, quitting when they earned the amount allowed.

Former Commissioner Apfel told me that he had had first-hand experience with the practice of working "up to the limit." The former commissioner said that his father, Walter Apfel, a steel salesman, continued to work after he retired in his early sixties and began collecting Social Security benefits.

"When my father retired," Apfel said, "he would work right up to the earnings limit—and not work beyond it—because he did not want to lose his Social Security benefit." The commissioner said he tried to convince his father that even if he worked beyond the limit, he would not be truly losing his benefits in the long run. "I'd say to him, 'Dad, you're going to get it back. You lose it for that year, but it gets added on to your benefits for the rest of your life.'" The former commissioner said his father was not convinced. "He'd say, 'I'm not sure what happens 10 or 15 years from now. I want to know what happens now.'"

One of the stumbling blocks to repealing the law was the initial cost of doing so. Partial repeal for the 65-to-69 age group was estimated to cost $20.4 billion over 10 years. Repeal for the younger group would have cost another $24.3 billion over 10 years. What finally made partial repeal happen was the growing budget surplus, a national labor shortage, and a fierce political battle for the votes of retirees and senior citizens in the year 2000. Advocates of repeal had argued that letting retirees work to their hearts' content would have beneficial economic and tax effects. They noted that retirees who keep working continue to contribute to Social Security and Medicare even though they are receiving retirement benefits. They also continue to pay income taxes.

One worker who rejoiced when Congress repealed the earnings limit was Antonio Santos, 68, a retired technician for Channel 4 in Dallas. Santos operates robotic cameras, a skill that is in heavy demand. Santos, who was unhappy with the earnings limit, said he tried to work fewer than 20 hours a week, but he wasn't always successful. In 1998, he recalled, he reached his earnings threshold by midyear and told his employer he would have to take the rest of the year off. However, when the TV station, where he'd worked for 45 years, desperately needed help, Santos said, he agreed to go in to work. That put him over the earnings limit. As a result, he had to give back part of his Social Security payments.

I talked to Santos on the day President Clinton signed the repeal bill. Santos was a happy man. "It's like a godsend for me. You can always use extra money when you're on a fixed retirement," he said. Being able to work part-time is important to him because it means that he doesn't have to dip into his savings.

"I think that if a person is willing to work and is in good health, there should be no limit on what that person can earn," Santos said. There were many in Washington who agreed: the House and the Senate both passed the repeal bill unanimously.

Worrying about the future

When I retired and began to learn about Social Security, I had two main questions. First, how does Social Security work? In this chapter, I've tried to provide some basic answers to that question.

Second, will Social Security still be around when my children and grandchildren retire? It would take a separate book to explore all the aspects of that question. Indeed, many such books have been written. But on the basis of what we know now, Social Security seems to be financially secure for the "short term," which covers the next three decades.

The 2009 report from the Social Security and Medicare boards of trustees tells us that the Social Security trust funds are "adequately financed" until 2037. This means that, until that year, there will be enough money coming into Social Security to pay 100 percent of the benefits due. After that, however, Social Security will begin to feel the effect of a shrinking workforce and a growing retiree force. As the years go on, fewer and fewer workers will be contributing to the system, while more and more workers will retire and stop contributing.

Today, there are 32 beneficiaries taking money out of the Social Security pool for every 100 workers putting money in. In 2008, the year that the baby boomers began to retire, there were 31 beneficiaries receiving payments for every 100 workers. By 2034, that number will rise to 47 beneficiaries per 100 workers, and in 2075, it will go up to 50 beneficiaries per 100 workers.

Social Security is America's most popular federal income program. For 74 years, its monthly payments have provided a safety net for the aged, widowed, and disabled. In fact, two-thirds of all beneficiaries receive more than half of their income from Social Security. For millions of widows, it is their only income. Though Social Security has its flaws, it has been dependable in good times and bad.

Thus, it is no surprise that politicians call Social Security the "third rail of politics," meaning: "Don't touch it or you will get burned." But the national image of Social Security as a bastion of certainty has begun to erode, and Social Security finds itself at the center of a fierce political debate over its future. The reason for the struggle is quite simple. The retirement of 78 million baby boomers, which began in 2008 and will continue for two decades, is creating a stressful financial situation for the government. Social Security is based on a pay-as-you-go system: payroll taxes paid into the system by today's workers are used to provide benefits to today's retirees. This system worked well when there were many more workers putting money in than taking money out. But as the boomers retire, fewer and fewer workers will be contributing to Social Security, while more and more workers will leave the workforce and stop contributing.

Figure 3.1 shows the expected decline in the number of workers for each Social Security beneficiary. From 3.7 workers in 1970, the number dropped to 3.2 in 2008 and will drop sharply to 2.0 workers in 2075. What this means is that if no changes are made to the Social Security system, the 74-year-old program faces a dire future. The 2009 report from the Social Security and Medicare boards of trustees predicted:

- In 2016, taxes paid into Social Security will fall short of the benefits paid out.
- In 2024, Social Security will have to start cashing in its government bonds to keep paying normal benefits.
- By 2037, those funds will run out.

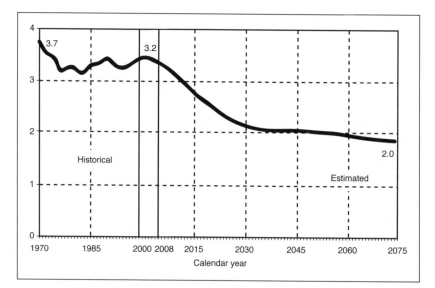

Figure 3.1   A look into the future.

Source: Social Security and Medicare Boards of Trustees 2009 Annual Reports.

After that, the payroll taxes being paid into Social Security will allow the agency to pay only 76 percent of its regular benefits. And that will drop to 73.9 percent in 2083.

What does all this mean for you and me? Since I am 82 and 2037 is 27 years away, my Social Security payments are likely to last at least as long as I do. However, unless Congress finds a way to shore up Social Security's finances, my children and grandchildren will get much smaller payments than I do.

My daughter, who was born in 1960, will reach her full retirement age of 67 in 2027. Thus, she would get full benefits for 10 years, until she was 77, and then would get partial benefits. My granddaughter, who was born in 1985, would reach her full retirement age of 67 in 2052, long after Social Security's assets had been depleted. Thus, she would get only partial benefits. And my other granddaughter, born in 1993, would reach 67 in 2060, when partial benefits would be moving up toward 78.1 percent. Faced with these projections, Washington's politicians, lawmakers, and policy experts agree that action is needed to solve Social Security's long-range financial problem. But they differ on how to do that.

President George W. Bush proposed a plan to allow workers to divert a portion of their Social Security payroll taxes to personal investment accounts. In an effort to deal with the long-term solvency problem, Bush also proposed reducing Social Security benefits for middle- and upper-income people while protecting the benefits of low-income Americans. The benefit reduction, Bush said, would make up 70 percent of Social Security's long-term deficit.

Bush's proposals, supported by many Republican lawmakers, were opposed by congressional Democrats, union leaders, and a number of public policy analysts. They argued that the so-called Social Security crisis was overblown and that, with minor fixes, the present system could remain solvent and continue to pay scheduled benefits.

Ideas for solving Social Security's financial problems included: raising the age for early retirement, which now begins at 62; shortening the 21-year period it will take for the full retirement age to move up from 65 to 67; raising the Social Security payroll tax to include wages above the current limit; and trimming retirement benefits for high-wage earners.

The personal accounts endorsed by Bush would have been voluntary and would have applied only to workers born in 1950 or later. Currently, workers pay 6.2 percent of their wages to Social Security. Bush would have permitted workers to divert 4 percent of their money to personal investment accounts. The money could have been invested in stocks, bonds, and other financial assets. The personal accounts would have supplemented a much-reduced Social Security benefit, and the size of a worker's retirement account would have depended on how well his or her investments performed.

The debate over the future of Social Security generated unusual intensity from individuals and organizations on all sides of the issues. President Bush made personal accounts the cornerstone of his second-term agenda and barnstormed the country to win public backing for his plan, which he said would allow workers to own their own accounts and pass them along to their heirs. Bush supporters mounted vigorous campaigns to promote personal accounts.

Opponents of the Bush plan were equally vocal. They included the 35-million-member AARP, the nation's largest senior citizen lobby, labor unions, and public interest groups. They argued that the Bush plan would destroy the family insurance concept of Social Security. Under the banner of reform, they said, the Bush plan would result in 20 to 30 percent cuts in future benefits for upper- and middle-income workers, thus turning Social Security into a welfare program for the poor. They also claimed that it was too risky to let workers invest their Social Security money in the stock market.

Democrats in Congress lined up solidly against the Bush plans. In fact, they declined to even discuss Social Security until Bush agreed to withdraw his plan for private accounts. Bush's second term ended without major changes to Social Security. And the 2008–2009 stock market crash reinforced the argument that allowing workers to put their Social Security savings into the financial markets was risky indeed.

During the early days of President Barack Obama's administration, the White House was heavily focused on its effort to win support for a national health-care reform plan. That put Social Security on the back burner. But the White House Web site made it clear that Obama was "committed to protecting Social Security." It also said, "The President stands firmly opposed to privatization and rejects the notion that the future of hard-working Americans should be left to the fluctuations of the financial markets."

For more information

The SSA publishes a number of booklets that explain the agency's retirement programs. The booklets, which are free, are available at your local SSA office; on the agency's Web site, www.socialsecurity.gov; or by calling 1-800-772-1213.

The following booklets are recommended for present and future retirees:

- *Understanding the Benefits* (Pub. 05-10024)
- *Retirement Benefits* (Pub. 05-10035)
- *How Work Affects Your Benefits* (Pub. 05-10069)
- *Fact Sheet: How Your Retirement Benefit Is Figured* (Pub. 05-10070)

DECISION 4

How should I take my pension payments?

Soon after I announced my retirement in the spring of 1996, I paid a visit to Michael C. Bahr, the benefits analyst in the *Washington Post*'s personnel department. For more than 20 years, Mike shepherded hundreds of employees through the retirement process, helping them make crucial decisions on how to deal with both their pensions and their 401(k) savings plans. Mike always made time to answer my questions about *Post* benefits.

Over the years, Mike and I had often chatted about the ups and downs of the stock market and the mutual funds that were offered to employees who were part of the newspaper's 401(k) savings plan. But I do not recall that we ever spent much time talking about the inner workings of the *Post*'s pension plan.

For one thing, the likelihood that I'd retire someday always seemed to be rather remote. Second, I had a sense that pension plans were very complicated, and I had no desire to strain my brain with information I wouldn't need for quite a while. So I never asked Mike to explain how the *Post* pension was calculated, although, looking back, I wish I had. It would have given me more time to think about my pension options before I retired.

Once a year, Mike sent *Post* employees a report that showed how much pension money each employee could expect to receive when he or she reached age 65. I recall that each year, as I looked at the figures in my report, I would think to myself, "That's not enough money to live on," and I would dismiss the idea of retiring.

Indeed, one of the reasons I worked until I was 69 was because I hoped that additional years on the job and a rising pay level would help improve my pension when I finally decided to take it. And that's exactly what happened.

Understanding your pension plan

There are, of course, two main types of pension plans: a defined benefit plan, which is paid for by the employer, and a defined contribution plan, such as a 401(k) savings plan, to which the employee, and often the employer, contribute.

The *Post*'s basic pension plan was a defined benefit plan. The *Post* paid all expenses; I put no money into it. The pension benefits I now receive were based on a formula that was, in turn, based on several factors, including the total number of years I worked at the paper, my average salary during my five highest paid years on the job, and the amount of money the company contributed to Social Security for me.

Using the *Post* formula, Mike figured out how much money I would get in my pension check each month if I took the maximum amount. He then told me I had several choices as to how I could take my monthly payments:

- A single life pension. This meant that I would receive my maximum pension of $2,532 a month, before deductions. But I could draw that pension check only during my lifetime. When I died, the pension would cease, and my wife would get nothing.
- A 50 percent spousal benefit. This meant that I could take a lower amount—about $2,160 a month for as long as I lived. After my death, my wife would receive half of my check, or $1,080 a month.
- A 100 percent spousal benefit. This meant that I would take an even lower benefit—about $1,900 a month, but upon my death, my wife would receive the same $1,900 check each month.

In other words, if I agreed to take less of a pension while I was alive, my spouse could continue to receive a pension check from the *Post* as long as she lived.

Making the pension decision

The question facing us was this: was it better—from both a financial and a commonsense point of view—to take my full pension or to take either the 50 percent or 100 percent spousal benefit? At the time I retired, Sara was already retired. And we were concerned that it might be difficult for us to go from living on two full salaries to living on a combination of pensions and Social Security income. Understandably, we felt that we would like to go into retirement with as much monthly income as possible.

This wasn't just a matter of greed. As I noted in an earlier chapter, I hadn't given much thought to my retirement budget. And it didn't look like our monthly living expenses would go down much when we retired. In fact, it seemed like they might go up. In short, because we hadn't planned carefully for our retirement budget, it seemed like we would need all the income we could get.

There were other factors, too. Sara, who had retired about two years earlier, was getting a pension of about $700 a month from GE. I also had more than $200,000 in life insurance. Our idea was that, if I died, Sara could invest the insurance money at a 6 percent interest rate and draw an annual income of $12,000, or $1,000 a month. That seemed like a good idea at the time, but $100,000 of my insurance consisted of a term life policy that eventually ran out and was too expensive to hang on to. Also, in the wake of the 2008–2009 market crash and recession, investing money at a 6 percent rate now seems like a distant dream. Fortunately, we both had modest 401(k) rollover accounts that she could draw on if I died.

But based on our original strategy at the time, it seemed to us that Sara would be protected financially if I took my maximum pension and left her no *Post* pension. So we did it. Sara signed off on the deal—something she was required to do by law. The federal government wants to be sure people are aware that if their spouses take a single life pension, they can be left without any pension income.

Having second thoughts

It is, of course, far too late to change my decision, although I must tell you that—13 years later—I am still having some second thoughts about the idea of taking my maximum pension payment and not leaving any pension for Sara. My second thoughts began to arise shortly after retirement when I decided to figure out how our family income would change upon my death. I added up how much money we were getting from pensions and Social Security. The total from pensions (after tax was withheld and after other deductions) was then $2,893. The total from Social Security was $2,600. The grand total was $5,493 a month. Since then, the numbers have improved somewhat—thanks mostly to Social Security's cost-of-living increases, which have raised our monthly benefits by 34 percent. Those benefits now total $3,478. Meanwhile, our pension payments, which are up by about 8 percent, total $3,139. The combined monthly total is $6,617.

But see how the picture changes if I die.

First, Sara would lose her $1,355 Social Security payment and get mine instead, because mine is higher. So she would get $2,123 a month from Social Security. Add her GE pension of $801 (after tax is withheld and after other deductions), and her grand total would be $2,932.

That's a big difference. In fact, it is a $3,685 difference between what we get together and what she'd get alone—a drop of 56 percent. How much income she could draw from my remaining $100,000 of life insurance and our 401(k) investments is, at this writing, problematical.

Sara's living expenses, as a single person, might be somewhat less than they are for the two of us together. But I think Sara's comfort level would be higher if she knew she would receive my pension for the rest of her life. Moreover, she wouldn't have to spend a lot of time managing investments or depending on others to do it for her. Nor would she have to worry about the health of the financial markets and whether her nest egg was being eroded.

So, after thinking about it, I have come to the conclusion that Sara would have been better off if I had taken the 100 percent spousal benefit. That would have given me a monthly check of

$1,900, and she would have continued to get the same check after I died. It would have been costly, of course: we would have given up $632 a month, and that would have made it harder for us to pay our bills. But it might have had advantages in future years.

Trying to outguess life

There is, of course, no way to know how long we are going to live; hence, speculating about what might happen in the future has its limitations. But let's try it, anyway.

Let's say when I retired at 69, I took the 100 percent spousal benefit of $1,900 a month. And let's say I lived for 10 years after retirement. By taking the $1,900 check instead of the full $2,532, I would have lost $632 a month, or $7,584 a year, or $75,840 for those 10 years.

If Sara then survived me for another 10 years, she would have gotten the same $1,900 a month check. So she would have gotten the same $75,840 over the 10 years. Essentially, we would have broken even. What I gave up, she would get back. But more than that, she would have had the security of knowing she was getting a regular pension check. And I think that's important.

Perhaps if I had thought all this through more carefully before I retired, I might have made a different decision on how to take my pension. The point of this story, though, is that the decision regarding how to take your pension is not a simple one: it has many more dimensions than I realized at the time I retired—and many more dimensions than you might realize.

Every pension plan is somewhat different. Therefore, every plan will have different options. For instance, the *Washington Post* plan did not offer a lump-sum option. But many pension plans do. Thus, you may have to choose between taking your pension in one lump sum or in monthly payments.

That lump-sum option has some pros and cons, which are summarized in one of my favorite reference books, *The Vanguard*

Guide to Investing During Retirement (New York: McGraw-Hill, 1998). Here they are.

Taking a lump-sum payment

PROS

Taking a lump sum enables you to make your own decisions on how you want to invest your money. As a result, you may be able to draw a higher income from your investments than you would get from a monthly pension check. The money also would be available for an emergency or a business opportunity. Monthly pension checks end when you die or when your spouse dies. But the lump-sum money, if wisely invested, would still be there for your heirs.

CONS

The temptation to spend all or some of your lump-sum money may be overwhelming. That's what happens to many people who get large amounts of money in lump-sum payments. Forty percent of workers aged 55 to 64 spend all or some of their lump-sum money, according to the U.S. Department of Labor. The other 60 percent put all their pension money into savings—a move that will help them pay for their living expenses in retirement. Moreover, the job of managing a large sum of money may involve more investment risk than you are either used to or comfortable with. And though you could derive more income from investing your money yourself, you also could get less if the investment climate is unfavorable. In addition, your lump-sum payment is likely to be fully taxable, which would give you a large tax bite in one year and thus reduce the amount of money you will have available to invest. However, you can postpone the taxes due on your lump-sum payment by rolling over the entire amount to an IRA. The money then can continue to grow on a tax-deferred basis until you are ready to take it out.

Taking a monthly payment

PROS

The process is simple: once you've decided on which option to choose—single life or a spousal benefit—the rest is automatic. You know how much you'll be getting each month, making it easy to draw up your retirement budget and to plan for taxes. Gyrations in the stock market or bond market won't be a worry, since your income is set. And if you're lucky enough to have a long retirement, those monthly payments will add up.

CONS

Pension plans generally are not adjusted for inflation. Thus, you could steadily lose purchasing power over the years. At an inflation rate of 3 percent, you would lose half your purchasing power in 24 years. And once you've taken your pension as a monthly payment—also called an annuity—you can't change it. Further, your pension ends when you die or when your spouse dies. That means there won't be any pension money to leave to your heirs.

In any event, Mike Bahr of the *Post* helped me put together a list of the things that a future retiree should think about before making pension decisions:

- Talk to the benefits expert in your company and ask for an explanation of the formula that your pension plan uses to determine how much money you will get when you retire. It may be possible to schedule your retirement in a way that will help you get a larger benefit. If, for instance, you expect a sizable pay raise in the next two years, it might be worth staying on the job to boost your average pay history—which could raise the amount of your pension.
- When talking to the benefits expert, get a copy of the various monthly payment options that will be available to you. Take time to study them, and think about the implications of giv-

ing up income now to leave income for your spouse in the future.

- Remember that your pension is considered by the IRS to be income and thus is fully taxable. Most pension plans will withhold taxes if you request that option. But, of course, tax withholding and deductions for health or life insurance will reduce the amount of money you will get in each check. Thus, in planning your retirement budget, use your "net" pension amount, not your gross amount.
- If you decide to roll over your lump-sum payment into an IRA, make sure that the rollover is made directly to the mutual fund, brokerage firm, or other company that you will choose for your IRA account. The most efficient way is to have your employer send the money directly to the company handling your account. That avoids taxes and penalties.

If you tell your employer to give you the money first—called an "indirect rollover"—the employer will withhold 20 percent for taxes, and you will have 60 days to open the IRA account, at which time you will have to make up the 20 percent from your own pocket. While you can get the 20 percent back eventually, you'll have to file a tax form to do so. So spare yourself that hassle by doing a direct rollover. Make the arrangements in advance with your company and the institution that you choose for your IRA.

- Before making any final decisions, consider the state of your health and that of your spouse. If you or your spouse have health problems that may shorten your normal longevity, consider those factors when making your pension choices.
- Consider, too, your overall financial situation, and try to choose a pension option that best fits that situation. If you take the maximum pension, as I did, will your spouse have enough other income coming in—or savings to draw on— to make ends meet when your pension stops? If you have limited savings, and you need Social Security and pension income

to support you, you may want to make sure that your spouse continues to get a pension check after your death, even if you have to take a lower monthly payment to do so.

- Think about your family obligations. Are there children or other relatives who depend on you for financial help? Those obligations may influence your decision regarding which pension payment option to take.

Finding a lost pension

Ordinarily, when you decide to retire and take your pension, all you need to do is to walk down the hall at work and talk to the benefits person. But suppose that after you've done that, you remember that 25 years ago you left a smaller company that also had a pension plan. Now that you're retiring, you wonder if you're entitled to a pension from your previous employer.

So you decide to call the company. You look in the phone book. The company is not listed. You call directory assistance. It doesn't have a listing either. You call the chamber of commerce. None of its people ever heard of the company. You do an Internet search. You try everything you can think of, but you can't find the company.

It doesn't seem like it would be that easy for a company to disappear. But it happens all the time, especially in the era of mergers and acquisitions. According to the Pension Benefit Guaranty Corporation (PBGC), a federal agency, "Thousands of retired workers in the United States are entitled to pension payments that they have not claimed because they do not know where to look."

As the PBGC points out in its useful booklet, *Finding a Lost Pension*, a company may:

- Move from one town to another
- Close a plant and consolidate its operations elsewhere
- Be bought by another company and be given a new name
- Merge with another company

- Divide into separate units, none of which keeps the original company name
- Go bankrupt
- Close its doors and go out of business

But even if a company has disappeared, it doesn't mean the company's pension plan also has disappeared. In many cases, the PBGC says, the money is sitting safely in a fund somewhere, waiting for the worker, or perhaps a surviving spouse, to come forward and claim it.

Helping people find "missing pensions" is one of the many responsibilities of the PBGC. The federal agency was created by the Employee Retirement Income Security Act of 1974 (ERISA) to encourage the continuation of defined benefit pension plans, provide timely and uninterrupted payment of pension benefits, and keep pension insurance premiums at a minimum. Currently, PBGC insurance protects the retirement benefits of 44 million workers. Because of that insurance, these workers will get their pensions even if their employer goes out of business or the plan runs out of money.

The PBGC's Pension Search program may help you locate a "missing" pension. But there are a couple of things you need to think about before you start looking. A key question is "Were you vested in the company's pension plan before you left the company?" Being vested means that no matter when you leave a job, you are eligible to receive a pension when you retire. If you weren't vested, you may not have a chance to claim benefits.

Today, most pension plans require five years of employment before vesting. Prior to the mid-1980s, plans typically required 10 years of service to vest. Prior to the mid-1970s, it was 20 years.

Also, before 1976, to get a pension you could be required to work for the same employer until you actually retired.

Indeed, from 1952 to 1971, I worked for a company in which you joined the pension plan at age 30, but you did not vest and thus could not get your pension until you retired at age 65, some 35 years later. If you left the company anytime before age 65, you got your own contribution back, plus 3 percent interest. And so, when I left the company at the age of 44, I lost about 14 years of pension benefits. Under ERISA, that type of plan is no longer permitted.

ERISA also created other broad protections that helped prevent workers from losing their pensions. The Department of Labor monitors pension plans to make sure that they are solvent and being managed properly. The Internal Revenue Service also regulates pension plans.

As mentioned earlier, the fact that a company has vanished doesn't mean that the pension plan has vanished, too. Many things could have happened to the plan. The PBGC notes that

- Despite reorganizations and mergers, the original plan may be intact. Those who run what today is left of the old company may still have a legal obligation to pay benefits due under the old plan.
- The plan may have bought an annuity from an insurance company, which undertook the obligation to pay annuities to everyone entitled to benefits under the plan.
- The plan may have been taken over by the PBGC, which will pay benefits up to certain limits.
- If a plan was terminated by the employer and benefits were paid to those employees who could be found, benefits for "missing" participants may have been turned over to PBGC for its Pension Search program.

So it may be possible for you to find your missing pension after all. However, it may take quite a bit of research. Suggestions on how to conduct a search for a missing pension are contained in the PBGC publication *Finding a Lost Pension.* For a free copy, write to Pension Benefit Guaranty Corporation, Communications and Public Affairs Department, 1200 K St. NW, Washington, D.C. 20005-4026. The information also is available on the Internet at www.pbgc.gov; on the home page, click on "About" and the "About" page will give you a choice of "PBGC Publications."

The PBGC's Web site also allows you to search electronically for a "missing" pension. You can search under your own name or under the company name. Click on the "Find Missing Participants" button on the PBGC Web page, www.pbgc.gov.

For more information

- The Pension Benefit Guaranty Corporation (PBGC). A government agency, the PBGC ensures that workers get their pension benefits and helps people find "lost pensions" (www.pbgc.gov).
- The U.S. Department of Labor. This agency's Web site offers information on pensions and other matters of interest to retirees (www.dol.gov).
- The Employee Benefit Research Institute (EBRI). A research and education group, EBRI seeks to enhance the development of sound employee benefit programs (www.ebri.org).
- American Savings Educational Council (ASEC). A coalition of public- and private-sector institutions, ASEC promotes savings and retirement planning (www.asec.org).
- AARP. The nation's largest organization for retirees and pre-retirees, AARP has a Web site that contains a wide range of pension-related information (www.aarp.org).

What should I do with the money in my company savings plan?

During the years that I worked at the *Washington Post*, I partici-
pated in the paper's 401(k) savings plan. This type of plan, offered
by many U.S. companies, was created by Uncle Sam to encourage
American workers to save for retirement and other financial goals.

These plans vary from company to company, but here is how
the plan worked at the *Post*.

As an employee, I set aside a portion of my salary for savings—
we were paid every two weeks—and the paper automatically
deposited that money into my account. In my later years at the
paper, I put about 9 percent of my pay into the 401(k) account.

The savings plan had several great features. To begin with, the
amount of money I earmarked for savings was deducted from my
pay before my income taxes were calculated and withheld. That
reduced my taxable earnings each payday and thus also reduced
my income taxes for the year. So, in a sense, I was doing two things
at once: saving money regularly and also saving on income taxes.
I thought that was a pretty good deal.

But it got even better. After I made my regular contribution to
the savings plan, the *Post* put in its contribution, called "a company match." In my later years at the paper, the match represented
4.5 percent of my pay, or about half of my contribution.

Finally, the paper gave me several choices about how I wanted
to invest the money in my account. I studied the list of available
funds and decided to put my contributions into the Vanguard
Windsor mutual fund, one of several stock funds that were offered
to *Post* employees. I also decided to use the company's matching
money to buy *Washington Post* stock.

Over the years, I have become convinced that the 401(k) plan
is a powerful way to save for retirement. It has several major
advantages:

• Your contribution goes directly into your savings plan before
  it is taxed. Thus, 100 cents of every dollar that you put into
  the plan goes to work. The contribution also reduces your
  income taxes for that year.

- The company's matching contribution is "free money" (although at some companies, the company match may be considered by management to be part of workers' overall benefits). In any event, the company contribution increases the amount of dollars that you have in your account. Those dollars also grow on a tax-deferred basis.

- Many companies let you invest your tax-deferred savings in mutual funds. That means your money will be managed by investment professionals who are likely to make your money grow over a period of years. Essentially, your money makes money—a wonderful bit of arithmetic called "compounding" that was so admired by Professor Albert Einstein, as noted in Chapter 2.

- No taxes are due on your savings or on any of the gains in your 401(k) plan until you begin to withdraw the money. However, as mentioned earlier, when you take out money that has not been taxed before, it will be taxed at ordinary income tax rates. In my case, I began to take money out of my account when I turned 70½, as required by the IRS. We'll talk about how to make your withdrawals in Chapter 6.

Looking back, I can see that being able to participate in the *Post*'s 401(k) plan for many years made a significant difference in the amount of money I had available for my retirement years. The same was true for Sara, who saved her money in a 401(k) plan at GE.

My gratitude for our 401(k) plans, however, does not change the warning I issued in Chapter 2 about the impact of taxes on retirees. While people should take maximum advantage of the 401(k) plan, they should also be aware that after they retire and begin to take money out of their tax-deferred savings accounts, they will pay income taxes on those withdrawals. They should set aside money to pay those taxes.

As Sara and I discovered, the tax bite can be rather large. Early in my retirement, it even became difficult to balance our family budget. I simply hadn't realized how much I would owe in taxes after taking money out of our 401(k) rollover accounts.

As mentioned earlier, if your income from pensions and Social Security totals $40,000 a year and you withdraw $10,000 from your IRAs, your total income will rise to $50,000. That is likely to increase your taxes for that year. Remember, however, that only a portion—up to 85 percent—of your Social Security benefits can be taxed each year.

Despite the tax aspect, Sara and I urge anyone who has the opportunity to contribute to a retirement savings plan at work to do so. Sign up as soon as you're eligible. Put in as much money as you can afford, up to the limit allowed by the plan. And in the year you reach your fiftieth birthday, begin making "catch up" contributions as well. If you are lucky, your plan will also include a new opportunity—namely, the ability to contribute after-tax dollars to a Roth 401(k) account instead of pre-tax contributions to the traditional 401(k) account. (You can contribute to one or both, but the combined total cannot exceed IRS limits.)

As you may know, there are no income eligibility limits for contributing to a Roth 401(k)—although there are limits for contributing to a regular Roth IRA. In the past, there have been income limits for conversions of traditional IRAs to Roth IRAs, but those limits have gone away in 2010.

So if you are concerned about possible increased tax rates in retirement, you may want to convert some or all of the assets in your traditional IRAs to Roth IRAs and pay the taxes due with assets you hold in a taxable investment account. Under a special rule, converting in 2010 will allow you to spread these taxes over two years: 2011 and 2012.

The main advantage of converting is that you won't have to withdraw funds from your Roth IRAs unless you want to, and even when you do, you won't have to pay income taxes on those withdrawals.

Turning workers into investors

For Sara and me, the 401(k) plan made it easy for us to save regularly and automatically year after year.

In the days before we had our 401(k) plans, we would take each paycheck and try to carve out a small piece for our savings account. Depending on how many bills we had on our desk, the money would sometimes get into our savings account and sometimes not.

With the advent of the 401(k) plan, our savings efforts were put on automatic pilot. The money came out of our paychecks regularly and silently, and it was difficult and potentially costly to access. We also got the benefit of matching money from our employers and tax-deferral from Uncle Sam.

That was the good news about contributing to our 401(k) plans. The bad news—if you want to call it that—was that once you put money into a plan, you also have to decide how you want to invest it. That sounds like it ought to be easy, but it's not: making your own investment decisions can be a considerable responsibility, especially as your nest egg grows over the years.

For instance, let's assume you earned $50,000 a year and put 6 percent of your salary ($250 a month) into your 401(k) plan. Your employer then matched half of your contribution with another $125 a month. That made the total contribution of $375 a month.

Let's also assume that you invested your savings in a Standard & Poor's (S&P) 500 mutual fund for 20 years, namely the decades of the 1980s and 1990s. During that period of time, the S&P 500's average annual total return was 11.2 percent a year, with dividends and capital gains reinvested. Thus, by the end of the 20 years, your 401(k) plan would have accumulated $333,332, less the expenses of the index fund.

My point is that people who may have known little about investing woke up one day and found themselves with extremely large amounts of money in their 401(k) plans, simply because they were fortunate to have steady, well-paying jobs for 15 or 20 years or more—during an era when the financial markets provided solid returns.

On the other hand, the markets do not always treat investors so favorably. After the financial tsunami of 2008–2009, market watchers began talking about "the lost decade" for stocks. They noted that as of the end of April 2009, the 10-year annualized return on the S&P 500 stock index was negative 2.5 percent. In other words, if you had invested in the S&P 500 in 1999 and looked at your investment 10 years later, you would have lost money.

While that kind of statistic can be discouraging, it also reminds investors that they have to carefully choose and monitor their investments through the years.

Meanwhile, thanks mainly to the 401(k) plan, the reality is that millions of American workers who otherwise might never have owned a stock or even a mutual fund are now "in the market" and have a stake in the performance of individual companies and the ups and downs of the financial markets. Those of us in the financial media—print, radio, and television—have seen an incredible growth in the audience for news and information about financial markets.

Of course, while investing in stocks and bonds offers you a chance to share in the long-term growth of the American economy, it also forces you to share in the market's short-term gyrations. On Wall Street, traders are fond of saying, "The market climbs a wall of worry." Individual investors, too, often have to climb that same wall. One of the great challenges of long-term investing is to learn enough about the markets and how they operate to be able to make intelligent investment decisions. We'll talk more about that in Chapter 7.

Meanwhile, I can testify that even people with knowledge of investing can act emotionally and make serious mistakes with their 401(k) money. I know because I did exactly that. This is my story.

My $70,000 investment mistake

In the 1980s, I was investing my 401(k) money in the Windsor Fund, a value-oriented stock mutual fund that was part of the Vanguard Group. The Windsor Fund was one of the investment choices offered to *Post* employees. The fund provided a respectable return. During the six years I was in the fund, it gained an average of 11.8 percent a year, and my savings grew nicely.

But in 1990, I got very nervous about the safety of my nest egg. On August 2, Iraq invaded Kuwait, and the international scene became very unsettled. I thought that a war might be in the offing. The markets also became very volatile. The Dow Jones Industrial Average dropped 18 percent between August 1 and October 11, 1990, on fears that the United States might get into a Middle East battle. At the same time, the price of the shares in the Windsor Fund fell from $12.39 to $9.72, a drop of 22 percent.

I was dismayed by the loss in the value of my Windsor shares and concerned about whether the downdraft would get worse. So I sold my shares and moved my money to a Vanguard money market fund. As it turned out, that was a bad mistake. In January 1991, when U.S. bombers struck Baghdad and returned without meeting significant resistance, the U.S. stock market came roaring back. The Dow ended 1991 with a gain of 20 percent, and the Windsor Fund rose 28.6 percent. By leaving the fund when I did, I got the fund's losses, and I wasn't there to get any of the fund's gains when the price of a share went back up.

That, unfortunately, is not the end of the story. Because of inertia or just a failure to pay attention to my financial affairs, I left my money in the money market fund for the next 5½ years until I retired. During those years, the money market fund earned a paltry average of 4.6 percent a year, while the Windsor Fund turned in an annualized gain of 18 percent a year.

I now figure that the decision to move my money out of the stock fund and into the money market fund—and leave it there for 5½ years—cost me about $70,000. True, it was money I never actually had in my pocket. But if I had left the money in the Windsor Fund, I would have retired with an extra $70,000.

Naturally, my wife and friends wanted to know how a financial writer who was knowledgeable about the markets could make that kind of mistake. I don't have a good answer. But I did learn a valuable lesson: don't try to outguess the market. Decide on your long-term investment strategy, and as long as it's the right strategy for you, stick to it.

The educated investor

When several of my friends heard about my $70,000 investment mistake, they tried to console me by confessing that they had made similar errors. "I know how you feel," they said. "I did the same thing myself." Frankly, it wasn't much consolation, but it was a reminder that millions of American workers are being called upon to make important investment decisions, often without much investment knowledge or experience.

Fortunately, there is a new national effort under way to expand "financial literacy" programs across the country. The objective is to teach millions of citizens how to manage and invest their money so that they can provide financial security for themselves and members of their family.

In 2008, President Bush created a President's Advisory Council on Financial Literacy, which was accompanied by an executive order declaring it to be "the policy of the federal government to encourage financial literacy among the American people."

Mr. Bush asked the 16-member council, headed by investment executive Charles R. Schwab, to help public and private organizations develop financial education programs for students and workers in U.S. industries.

The White House recognition of the need to increase "financial literacy" was a pat on the back for several national organizations that have been working for many years to bring financial education to high schools and colleges.

In the council's first annual report, Schwab wrote:

> We believe the market turmoil and credit crisis of 2008 underscore the critical need for improved financial literacy in the United States. Far too many Americans entered into home and other loan agreements that they did not understand and ultimately could not afford. More broadly, the lack of basic skills such as how to create and maintain a budget, understand credit, or save for the future, are preventing millions of Americans from taking advantage of our vibrant economic system.

Choosing what to do with your money when you retire

When you walk into the office of the benefits specialist at your company and announce that you are ready to retire, the specialist will tell you that you have several options on what to do with the money you have saved in your 401(k) plan.

If you have worked for 20 years or more, have been saving aggressively and investing thoughtfully, the amount in your savings account may be the largest pot of money you've ever had. If that is the case—and I hope it is—you will want to consider your options very carefully. Assuming you are over 59½, those options include the following.

A rollover IRA

This is the option that Sara and I both chose when we retired. Before Sara left GE, she opened an IRA rollover account at a major mutual fund company. At that time, GE sent her a check for her 401(k) money that was made out to her and to the mutual fund company (which indicated that the money had to go into her account at the fund company). Sara quickly took the check to the local office of the fund company and deposited the money into her account.

If she were doing it today, she'd fill out the paperwork requesting a "trustee-to-trustee transfer" and avoid the need to be the "middle man." Initially, she parked the money in a money market account. Afterward, she studied the available mutual funds and invested portions of her money in some of those funds. Her objective was to keep the money invested and to keep it working and growing.

When I retired from the *Post* a few years later, I did much the same thing. I opened an IRA rollover account at a major brokerage firm, and the *Post* sent me a check for my 401(k) money made out to me and to the brokerage company. I then deposited the check in my new rollover account, also initially in a money market fund. I chose a brokerage account because I wanted to invest in specific stocks rather than funds.

Over the past few years, I have had my share of winners and losers in the stock market, but, like Sara, I achieved my main purpose, which was to keep the money invested and growing.

What happens to our savings is of great concern to us because we know we will have to depend on our 401(k) money to help pay for some of our retirement expenses in the years ahead.

Doing a rollover IRA, I believe, was the best way to deal with our 401(k) money. But there are other options, as well. A word of caution: if, despite recent market events, you have a significant amount of highly appreciated company stock in your retirement plan portfolio, you may wish to take advantage of a special tax break available to you. This is described in detail later in this chapter.

Indirect rollover IRA

In this scenario, your employer sends you a check made out just to you for your 401(k) money. But the employer is required to withhold 20 percent of your money for income taxes—money that gets sent to the IRS. For instance, if you have $200,000 in your account, your employer will withhold $40,000 for the IRS and send you a check for $160,000. You will then have 60 days to open an IRA rollover account somewhere and deposit your money.

To avoid income taxes, you will be required to deposit the full $200,000 in your IRA rollover account. That means you will have to come up with the $40,000 your employer withheld for taxes out of your own pocket. If you don't, this amount will be treated as a taxable distribution. Eventually, you may be able to get your $40,000 back when you file your federal income tax return for the year of the distribution.

In short, the indirect rollover produces the same result as the direct rollover, but it comes with a lot of hassle for very little gain. About the only benefit of this strategy is that you have use of 80 percent of the money from your employer's plan for a maximum of 60 days. Under most circumstances, it hardly seems worth the trouble.

Whether you roll over your assets directly or indirectly to an IRA, the money in your 401(k) plan represents the money you and your employer put there, plus any gains on your investments. These sums are considered pretax money, meaning money that has yet to be taxed. However, if you contributed any additional money to your company account—money on which you already paid taxes—it, too, may be rolled over to an IRA, or you may choose to take those assets and keep them in a taxable account for emergencies.

A cash distribution

Taking all of your savings out of your plan without rolling them over to an IRA is probably the worst thing you can do with your 401(k) money because you will simply give up most of it in taxes. Here is an example of what can happen to your $200,000 if you take it all in cash:

• First, your company will withhold 20 percent for taxes, or $40,000 for the IRS.

• Second, let's assume that the cash distribution puts you in the 33 percent marginal income tax bracket. Your employer has already withheld 20 percent. So you could owe another 13 percent of $200,000, or $26,000, if you withdraw the lump sum in one year.

• Third, in addition to paying federal taxes, you will have to remit state and/or local taxes on your withdrawal. Suppose that these taxes cost you another 7 percent, or $14,000.

That all adds up to $80,000, leaving you only $120,000 from your original $200,000. That doesn't sound like a good way to handle money that you carefully saved for so many years.

But perhaps the most devastating effect of taking a cash distribution is that all of your remaining money loses its tax-deferred status and becomes fully taxable, which can be costly over the long term. The dramatic difference between what a tax-deferred $200,000 will produce and what a taxable $124,000 will produce over long periods of time is shown in Table 5.1.

Table 5.1 Why It's *Not* a Good Idea to Take Your 401(k) Money in Cash

Time Period	Growth of $200,000 Rollover Investment (Pretax Balances)*	Growth of $124,000 Cash Investment (After-Tax Balances)
10 years	$431,785	$201,983
15 years	$634,434	$257,787
20 years	$932,191	$329,009

*The rollover account will grow on a tax-deferred basis and assumes an average annual return of 8 percent. The after-tax lump sum is assumed to grow at an after-tax return of 5 percent.

Leaving money in your 401(k) plan

Some 401(k) plans will permit you to leave your money in the plan, some will not. Federal regulations say a company may make you roll over your assets to an IRA if you have less than $5,000 in your account when you leave the company. In many cases, I am told, you can stay in your plan if you have at least $5,000 there. Since your decision to leave your employer's plan will be irrevocable, it is important to consult with a financial advisor before making your decision.

If you happen to be someone who plans to continue working part-time in a profession like medicine where you are more likely to be exposed to litigation, you might want to leave your assets in the plan, where they may be better protected from creditors than if they are held in an IRA. This varies from state to state, so check with your attorney if you are concerned. Fees might be lower by leaving your assets in the plan. And in rare cases, you may continue to have opportunities to take loans from your account, even after you have left employment. Finally, if you plan to continue working for your company after age 70½, you will probably be able to delay taking required minimum distributions from your plan account until the year after you finally retire. (If you have rolled the assets over to an IRA, however, required minimum distributions are mandatory even if you continue employment with your old employer.)

Dealing with company stock

If your 401(k) plan allowed you to invest in company stock, you have several options. You can sell the stock within your 401(k) plan, if that is permitted, and roll the total amount of money from your plan into an IRA rollover account, either directly or indirectly. Or, you can keep the shares of stock and roll them over into an IRA account, along with any other money in your plan.

However, you may have company stock in your plan that has substantially increased in value over the years. (Indeed, let's hope you do!) If so, to benefit from special tax treatment, you may want to consider moving the stock to a taxable brokerage account at the same time you roll over the balance of your 401(k) into an IRA, suggests senior financial planner Christine S. Fahlund at T. Rowe Price Investment Services.

To be eligible for this special tax treatment, your one-time distribution from your employer plan must qualify as a "lump sum distribution," so be sure to check with your plan administrator before taking action.

This strategy enables you to pay capital gains taxes on the appreciation when you sell your employer stock. The capital gains taxes may be considerably less than the amount you would have to pay in ordinary income taxes when you withdraw assets from your rollover IRA account during retirement. The details get a bit tricky, but stay with me.

At the time the shares are taken from your 401(k) plan, you will pay ordinary income taxes only on the original cost basis of the shares, not on their fair market value. If you decide to sell right away some of the shares that you deposit into the brokerage account, you would pay capital gains taxes (currently at a 5 percent or 15 percent rate) on the total long-term gains realized since the shares were purchased in the plan. However, before selling shares of the stock that have appreciated further since that deposit date, you should hold those shares at least an additional year in the brokerage account. The reason for applying this holding strategy is to avoid having those new gains treated as short term and taxed at ordinary income tax rates.

If you never sell the shares, the tax advantages get even better, Fahlund says. This is what would happen: When your heirs sell the shares, they will not pay capital gains tax on any gains that occurred between the time you moved the shares to the brokerage account and the date of your death. That is because when you die, the cost basis of the shares is "stepped up"—as tax people like to say. This means that, for your heirs, the cost basis of your shares will be the price of the shares on the day you died. Thus, if they sell the shares immediately, they will pay capital gains taxes only on the appreciation that occurred while the shares were still in your 401(k) account.

All in all, the 401(k) plan is like a good friend. It'll be there when you need it. But as with any friend, take time to get to know it well, and treat it with respect.

Saving in America: good news and bad

The good news is that the savings rate in America, after being negative for many years, rose to 6.9 percent in May 2009, the highest point in 15 years.

The bad news is that many people are now saving for the following reasons:

- The 2008–2009 market crash erased $2 trillion from workers' retirement savings.
- The national unemployment rate has risen to almost 10 percent, and almost 15 million Americans are out of work.
- Because of the housing bust, home values plummeted, leaving many homeowners "under water"—owing more on their mortgages than their houses are worth.
- Because of job losses and falling home prices, millions of Americans lost their homes to foreclosure.
- The national business recession and "jobless recovery" may extend until 2011 and 2012.

Simply put, Americans seem to be saving out of fear of spending any money that they don't have to spend. The national recession and personal financial losses also affected the way baby boomers were thinking about their futures. An AARP study showed that 27 percent of all workers age 45 and older decided to postpone their plans to retire.

Under the circumstances, delaying retirement made sense for many boomers. At 65, they become eligible for Medicare. If they left their jobs before 65 and lost their company insurance, they might have had to pay privately for health insurance.

Also, by working past full retirement age, now generally 66, they earn an 8 percent bonus for each year that they delay taking benefits. At 70, they get a 32 percent bonus and are thus able to collect their maximum monthly Social Security payment.

Also, staying on the job allows the boomers to continue to draw their salaries and put money into their 401(k) plans for a few more years. That also might give their 401(k) investments time to recover from some of their losses.

If there is any irony to be found in the sudden boom in the national savings rate, it is that it follows years of surveys showing that American workers are not saving enough and are ill-prepared financially for retirement. In the 2008 Retirement Confidence Survey conducted by the Employee Benefit Research Institue (EBRI) and Mathew Greenwald & Associates, 49 percent of those surveyed said their savings and investments totaled less than $25,000, not counting the value of their homes or future pensions. Even more alarming perhaps, 61 percent of workers said their savings and investments totaled less than $50,000. And many of these workers were only a few years from retirement age.

Whether the current surge in the national savings rate will continue is uncertain but, as of this writing, people who are trying hard to save for retirement are facing extraordinary financial challenges.

For more information

BOOKS

Larimore, Taylor, Mel Lindauer, and Michael LeBoeuf, *The Boglehead's Guide to Investing*, New York: Wiley, 2006.

Morris, Virginia B., and Kenneth M. Morris, *Standard & Poor's Guide to Money and Investing,* New York: McGraw-Hill, 2005.

O'Neill, William, *How to Make Money in Stocks: A Winning System in Good Times and Bad,* 4th Edition, New York: McGraw-Hill, 2009.

Ruffenach, Glenn, and Kelly Greene, *The Wall Street Journal. Complete Retirement Guidebook. How to Plan It, Live It and Enjoy It,* New York: Three Rivers Press, 2007.

When do I have to take money out of my IRAs?

When I reached my seventieth birthday, my family and friends had a party to help me celebrate. Six months later, when I turned 70½, the only people celebrating were those at the IRS.

As mentioned earlier, the year you turn 70½ is when you are required by Uncle Sam to start withdrawing money from your IRAs and most other tax-deferred retirement accounts. (Roth IRAs are not included.) And, of course, you have to pay income taxes on some or all of that money. It's no wonder the tax collectors were so happy when I turned 70½. They had waited 20 years for those taxes.

For most of us, paying taxes on IRA withdrawals is a good-news, bad-news story. The good news is that we were wise to save money in tax-deferred retirement accounts for a long time. The bad news is that when it's time to take the money out, most or all of it will be taxable. In my case, it means that for every dollar I take out of my IRAs and spend, I have to take an extra 25 cents out of my non-IRA savings to pay my federal and state taxes.

That hurts, especially if you didn't anticipate that expense when you worked out your retirement budget. Unfortunately, I didn't. But hopefully, if you save regularly while you're working and invest wisely, you should be able to pay your taxes and have money left over to help pay your living expenses.

However, whether you save a lot of money or a little money in a retirement account, the process of taking the money out—as Uncle Sam requires—will strain your brain. Of course, it helps to know the lingo. In the language used in the IRS regulations, withdrawals from IRAs are called distributions. And the whole process of withdrawing money from retirement accounts at 70½ is known as taking your required minimum distributions (RMDs).

Thus, if you run into a friend on the street who asks: "Have you taken your RMDs yet?" be assured that your friend is not asking about whether you've taken your vitamins recently—only whether you've made your IRA withdrawals yet.

Curiously, some mutual funds and financial companies use the phrase "minimum required distributions" (MRDs) while others use "required minimum distributions" (RMDs). Why? Nobody seems to know. But I'm going to go with the IRS version—RMDs. After all, I say, "A tax by any other name is still a tax."

The rules

Most taxpayers will have to consult only one simple IRS table each year—the Uniform Lifetime Table (Table 6.1)—to find the number they need to calculate their withdrawals. Most IRA owners will use that table.

There is, however, one exception: in a case where your spouse is the sole beneficiary of your IRA for the entire year and your spouse is also more than 10 years younger than you are, the two of you will use a different IRS table to calculate your withdrawal. It's called the Joint Life and Last Survivor Expectancy Table (Table 6.2).

Although the IRS has simplified the RMD withdrawal process, there are still some aspects that are complicated—especially when they involve beneficiaries. For instance, if you leave your IRA assets to your grandchildren or even great grandchildren, this is a likely scenario: if the custodian retains the assets in "an inherited IRA," the custodian, or eventually the young heirs themselves, need withdraw only their basic RMD amounts each year, based on their actuarial life expectancies. That could be 80 years or more (from the IRS Single Life Expectancy Table). That process can stretch out the tax-deferred growth potential of much of their inheritance for many years—although they can always withdraw more or actually deplete the account at any time.

But while you are still dealing with your own required withdrawals, be careful to take the right amount. While you are allowed to take out more than the minimum, you'd better not take less, or you could wind up paying a hefty penalty to the IRS: 50 percent of the difference between the amount of money you withdrew and the amount that you should have withdrawn. And then, after paying the penalty, you must still withdraw the correct amount and pay any tax and interest due on that amount.

I therefore strongly recommend that you consult a financial planner or an accountant before you begin your withdrawals. This is particularly true if you have large sums of money in your retirement plans.

Making your first withdrawal

When it comes to taking your first withdrawal, you have two options. The first is to take your withdrawal in the year in which you are 70½. Or, if you wish, you can wait until April 1 of the following year for the initial withdrawal and then take a second withdrawal by December 31 of that year.

However, taking two withdrawals in the same year means that you will pay income taxes on two withdrawals instead of one. I elected to take my first withdrawal when I was 70½ because I did not want to pay income taxes on two withdrawals in one year.

If you take your withdrawal in the year in which you turn 70½, you will base it on how much money you had in your retirement accounts as of the previous December 31. As an example, let's say you reach 70½ in 2010. If you take your withdrawal in 2010, it will be based on the amount of money in your accounts on December 31, 2009.

If you want to wait, you must take your first withdrawal by April 1, 2011. If you do that, the withdrawal will still be based on your account total as of December 31, 2009. However, if you do wait, you will then have to take a second withdrawal before December 31, 2011. In this case, the second withdrawal would be based on the amount of money in your accounts as of December 31, 2010.

Making a list

When you get close to 70½, it's a good time to ask yourself: "How many IRAs or other tax-deferred accounts do I have?" That's an important question because, when you make your withdrawals, you have to consider the assets in all of those accounts. (Roth IRAs are not included.)

Here are some of the tax-deferred accounts that must be considered.

TRADITIONAL IRAs

A traditional IRA is a tax-deferred savings account for people who earn income. If you earn income, you also may contribute to a traditional IRA for a nonworking spouse. Contributions to traditional IRAs can be either deductible or nondeductible. A deductible contribution is so named because you were able to take an income tax deduction for the money you put into that account. The amount you put in, together with any earnings on those investments, is taxable when you begin to take money out of that account. A nondeductible contribution is a contribution that you made with after-tax money. You did not receive a tax deduction when you made the contribution. Thus, only the investment earnings portion of each distribution is taxable.

IRA ROLLOVER ACCOUNTS

These are accounts that you set up when you roll over money from your 401(k) or similar retirement plan to an IRA account at a bank, brokerage, or mutual fund company.

SIMPLIFIED EMPLOYEE PENSION PLAN (SEP-IRA)

This is a retirement plan for sole proprietors, partners, or corporations. A SEP is set up as an individual employee retirement account, and the employer makes contributions to each separate account.

SAVINGS INCENTIVE MATCH PLAN FOR EMPLOYEES (SIMPLE-IRA)

A SIMPLE-IRA is a retirement plan for the self-employed or for a partnership or corporation with up to 100 employees. Employees can make pretax contributions from their pay; employers must make matching or nonmatching contributions.

Defined contribution plans (including profit-sharing and money purchase plans)

In 2009, the most money that could be contributed to a defined contribution account was $49,000, including both employer and employee contributions. For example, an employee could contribute 100 percent of his salary up to $16,500 (plus an additional catch-up contribution of $5,500 if 50 or older). The employer could contribute an additional 25 percent of salary, with the total not to exceed the overall maximum of $49,000.

Company 401(k) plan

If an employee who retires leaves money in a company 401(k) plan, when the individual reaches 70½, he or she must begin to withdraw money from the retirement account [this includes Roth 401(k) money]. The rules of a particular 401(k) or Roth 401(k) plan may affect how the withdrawals can be made. On the other hand, if you are still working for that employer in the year you reach 70½, you do not need to begin taking required distributions until April 1 of the calendar year following the year in which you ultimately retire from the company.

403(b) plan

The 403(b) plan is generally available to employees of tax-exempt organizations such as colleges, universities, hospitals, and charitable groups. Certain mandatory withdrawal rules apply to these plans as well.

Don't give up yet

Once you have figured out how many tax-deferred accounts you own, make a list of those accounts and your balances as of the previous December 31. The next step is to find out how much money you must take out of each account in the first year of your RMDs.

To do that, you will have to use one of two IRS life expectancy tables that will show you the divisor to use when you figure out your withdrawals. These two tables are the Uniform Lifetime Table (Table 6.1) and the Joint Life and Last Survivor Expectancy Table (Table 6.2).

The IRS's goal is to make sure you take out some of your retirement money each year and pay the income taxes due on that money. If you die before the end of your withdrawal period, your beneficiary may have the option to continue withdrawing annual payments from the account beginning in the year following your death. Note that your beneficiary, like you, can always take more, but never less, than the minimum required amount each year. Otherwise, penalties will apply.

When a husband dies, his widow-beneficiary can roll over the IRA into her own IRA and use the favorable Uniform Lifetime Table (Table 6.1).

To use Table 6.1, locate your age. The number next to your age will be the divisor. If you are using Table 6.2, use your age and the age of your beneficiary to locate your divisor.

Table 6.1   Uniform Lifetime Table*

Your Age	Your Factor	Your Age	Your Factor
70	27.4	86	14.1
71	26.5	87	13.4
72	25.6	88	12.7
73	24.7	89	12.0
74	23.8	90	11.4
75	22.9	91	10.8
76	22.0	92	10.2
77	21.2	93	9.6
78	20.3	94	9.1
79	19.5	95	8.6
80	18.7	96	8.1
81	17.9	97	7.6
82	17.1	98	7.1
83	16.3	99	6.7
84	15.5	100	6.3
85	14.8		

*For use by owners of IRAs.
Source: Internal Revenue Service.

Table 6.2   Joint Life and Last Survivor Expectancy Table*

Your Present Age

Spousal Beneficiary Age	70	71	72	73	74	75	76	77	78	79	80	81	82	83	84	85
50	35.1	35	34.9	34.8	34.8	34.7	34.6	34.6	34.5	34.5	34.5	34.4	34.4	34.4	34.3	34.3
51	34.3	34.2	34.1	34	33.9	33.8	33.8	33.7	33.6	33.6	33.6	33.5	33.5	33.5	33.4	33.4
52	33.4	33.3	33.2	33.1	33	33	32.9	32.8	32.8	32.7	32.7	32.6	32.6	32.6	32.5	32.5
53	32.6	32.5	32.4	32.3	32.2	32.1	32	32	31.9	31.8	31.8	31.8	31.7	31.7	31.7	31.6
54	31.8	31.7	31.6	31.5	31.4	31.3	31.2	31.1	31	31	30.9	30.9	30.8	30.8	30.8	30.7
55	30.3	30.9	30.8	30.6	30.5	30.4	30.3	30.3	30.2	30.1	30.1	30	30	29.9	29.9	29.9
56	29.5	30.1	30	29.8	29.7	29.6	29.5	29.4	29.3	29.3	29.2	29.2	29.1	29.1	29	29
57	28.8	29.4	29.2	29.1	28.9	28.8	28.7	28.6	28.5	28.4	28.4	28.3	28.3	28.2	28.2	28.1
58	28.1	28.6	28.4	28.3	28.1	28	27.9	27.8	27.7	27.6	27.5	27.5	27.4	27.4	27.3	27.3
59		27.9	27.7	27.5	27.4	27.2	27.1	27	26.9	26.8	26.7	26.6	26.6	26.5	26.5	26.4
60		27.2	27	26.8	26.6	26.5	26.3	26.2	26.1	26	25.9	25.8	25.8	25.7	25.6	25.6
61			26.3	26.1	25.9	25.7	25.6	25.4	25.3	25.2	25.1	25	24.9	24.9	24.8	24.8
62				25.4	25.2	25	24.8	24.7	24.6	24.4	24.3	24.2	24.1	24.1	24	23.9
63					24.5	24.3	24.1	23.9	23.8	23.7	23.6	23.4	23.4	23.3	23.2	23.1

Age											
64	23.6	23.4	23.2	23.1	22.9	22.8	22.7	22.6	22.5	22.4	22.3
65		22.7	22.5	22.4	22.2	22.1	21.9	21.8	21.7	21.6	21.6
66			21.8	21.7	21.5	21.3	21.2	21.1	21	20.9	20.8
67				21	20.8	20.6	20.5	20.4	20.2	20.1	20.1
68					20.1	20	19.8	19.7	19.5	19.4	19.3
69						19.3	19.1	19	18.8	18.7	18.6
70							18.5	18.3	18.2	18	17.9
71								17.7	17.5	17.4	17.3
72									16.9	16.7	16.6
73										16.1	16
74											15.4

* Use this table to determine your life expectancy factor only if your sole primary beneficiary is a spouse who is more than 10 years younger than you are. To determine your 2010 RMD, divide your year-end retirement account balance as of December 31, 2009, by the divisor in the table above that corresponds to your age and your spouse's age as of December 31, 2010. For example, if you will be age 73 as of December 31, 2010 and your spouse will be age 62 as of that date, the life expectancy factor used to calculate your 2006 RMD would be 25.4.

Source: The Vanguard Group.

To calculate your withdrawals, divide the amount of money in each of your retirement accounts by your divisor. That's where your list will come in handy. The IRS says that you must do the calculation for each of your accounts.

For IRAs and 403(b) accounts, here's how it works: if you own four deductible IRAs, or four 403(b) accounts, each with balances of $20,000 as of December 31, 2009, and your withdrawal factor is 26.2, you will have to withdraw a minimum of $763 from each of the four accounts, or a total of $3,052. You may take the money out of one IRA account or more than one IRA account. In turn, if you have 403(b) accounts, you may take all of the money out of one 403(b) account as well. You may not combine 403(b) and IRA balances, however.

Now, let's assume you have a fifth IRA—a nondeductible one. You contributed $10,000 in after-tax dollars to this account. Over the years, it gained another $10,000, for a total of $20,000. Under IRS rules, the $10,000 you contributed is not taxable.

So what do you do? Under this scenario, according to financial planner Christine S. Fahlund at T. Rowe Price Investment Services, you must total up the value of all your IRA accounts or the value of all your 403(b) accounts. In this case, the total is $100,000 (five accounts of $20,000 each). Then you have to figure out what portion of your withdrawals is not taxable.

Here's how the arithmetic goes: of the $100,000 in your accounts, $10,000, or 10 percent, was contributed in after-tax money. We already know that you have to withdraw $763 from each account for a total of $3,815 (five accounts multiplied by $763). However, only 90 percent is taxable.

For each of the $763 withdrawals, you would have to pay taxes on only $687. Thus, for the five accounts, the total taxable amount of the withdrawals would be $3,435 (five accounts multiplied by $687). The other $380 comes out income tax free.

When I made my first IRA withdrawal, I tried to be careful to take the right amount so that I would not be penalized for taking out less than required. You, too, should be careful.

How to use the life-expectancy tables

As I noted, the IRS gives you two tables to help you figure out your withdrawals. The IRS also provides a third table that is intended for use by your beneficiaries after your death.

Here is a rundown on how all three of these tables are to be used (using a $100,000 IRA as an example).

Table 6.1 is the Uniform Lifetime Table. It is the table that will be used by most individuals who must withdraw money from their IRAs and tax-deferred accounts.

At age 70½, assuming your seventieth birthday was in the current calendar year, your divisor would be 27.4. Divide $100,000 by 27.4, and you get $3,649, the amount of your initial minimum withdrawal. In the following year, when you celebrate your seventy-first birthday, you return to the Uniform Lifetime Table and select the new divisor, 26.5, and divide that figure into your new December 31 balance to obtain the amount of your RMD in year two.

Table 6.2 is the Joint Life and Last Survivor Expectancy Table. This should be used in cases where your spouse is the sole beneficiary of your account and is more than 10 years younger than you are.

For instance, if you are 73 and your spouse is 62—11 years younger—the table shows that your divisor is 25.4. If your account is worth $100,000, your first-year minimum withdrawal would be $100,000 divided by 25.4, or $3,937. In each year thereafter, the two of you go back to the Joint Life and Last Survivor Expectancy Table and find your new divisor and divide that factor into your new December 31 balance. After the first spouse dies, the surviving spouse rolls over the IRA to her own name and then takes RMDs in future years using a factor based solely on her own age found in the Uniform Lifetime Table.

Table 6.3, the Single Life Expectancy Table, is used mostly by nonspouse beneficiaries. Let's say that John, 74, dies when his daughter, Mary, is 41. Mary is John's beneficiary on his IRA account. In the year following John's death, Mary, now 42, consults

Table 6.3   Single Life-Expectancy Table*

Age	Life Expectancy	Age	Life Expectancy
0	82.4	39	44.6
1	81.6	40	43.6
2	80.6	41	42.7
3	79.7	42	41.7
4	78.7	43	40.7
5	77.7	44	39.8
6	76.7	45	38.8
7	75.8	46	37.9
8	74.8	47	37.0
9	73.8	48	36.0
10	72.8	49	35.1
11	71.8	50	34.2
12	70.8	51	33.3
13	69.9	52	32.3
14	68.9	53	31.4
15	67.9	54	30.5
16	66.9	55	29.6
17	66.0	56	28.7
18	65.0	57	27.9
19	64.0	58	27.0
20	63.0	59	26.1
21	62.1	60	25.2
22	61.1	61	24.4
23	60.1	62	23.5
24	59.1	63	22.7
25	58.2	64	21.8
26	57.2	65	21.0
27	56.2	66	20.2
28	55.3	67	19.4
29	54.3	68	18.6
30	53.3	69	17.8
31	52.4	70	17.0
32	51.4	71	16.3
33	50.4	72	15.5
34	49.4	73	14.8
35	48.5	74	14.1
36	47.5	75	13.4
37	46.5	76	12.7
38	45.6	77	12.1

Table 6.3   Single Life-Expectancy Table*

Age	Life Expectancy	Age	Life Expectancy
78	11.4	95	4.1
79	10.8	96	3.8
80	10.2	97	3.6
81	9.7	98	3.4
82	9.1	99	3.1
83	8.6	100	2.9
84	8.1	101	2.7
85	7.6	102	2.5
86	7.1	103	2.3
87	6.7	104	2.1
88	6.3	105	1.9
89	5.9	106	1.7
90	5.5	107	1.5
91	5.2	108	1.4
92	4.9	109	1.2
93	4.6	110	1.1
94	4.3	111+	1.0

*For use by beneficiaries.
Source: Internal Revenue Service.

the table and finds that, based on her current age, her divisor is 41.7, meaning that she can take withdrawals from John's IRA account for more than 40 years. If the account balance was $100,000 on December 31 of the year of John's death, Mary's first minimum withdrawal would be $2,398 ($100,000 divided by 41.7). She can always take more than the RMD amount in any given year. In the second year, Mary does not need to go back to the Single Life-Expectancy Table. Instead, she subtracts one year from her RMD factor, or divisor, of 41.7 to arrive at her new factor of 40.7 and divides her new December 31 ending balance by that factor. The following year, her factor would be 39.7, and so forth.

Summing up

Well, those are the bare bones of the process for taking IRA withdrawals. If you are embarking on this process, my advice is to start early, study your options carefully, and get all the advice you can find. You'll get through it. Then, along with me, you will wonder: why is retirement such hard work?

For more information

The IRS life-expectancy tables are contained in IRS publication No. 590, *Individual Retirement Arrangements.* To order the booklet, call 1-800-829-3676. You can also download the publication from the IRS Web site: www.irs.gov.

Vanguard offers an RMD (required minimum distribution) kit, which is available on its Web site: www.vanguard.com (under forms) or by calling Vanguard Retail Services: 1-800-662-7447.

The T. Rowe Price Web site has a section devoted to the topic of RMDs, with tools to help you estimate the amount you may need to withdraw and to set up an automated RMD program for IRAs held at T. Rowe Price. You can find this information at www.troweprice.com/rmd.

T. Rowe Price also publishes the *T. Rowe Price Guide for IRA and 403(b) Account Beneficiaries.* It explains the options available to beneficiaries who inherit these accounts. It can be downloaded from the Web site mentioned above (www.troweprice.com/rmd).

DECISION 7

How should I invest during retirement?

Three years after I retired, I was shocked to discover that if my wife and I didn't cut down on our spending and get better results on our investments, we would use up all our retirement savings within eight years. As you can imagine, that was extremely bad news, because at that point, I was only 72 and my wife, Sara, was 70. In eight years, I would be only 80 and Sara would be 78—not terribly old by today's standards. In fact, Sara and I have many friends who are 80 and older and still lead active, interesting lives.

The truth of the matter is that I was hoping our savings would last until we were in our nineties. But my calculations told me we would fall far short of that goal.

Now, I'm not suggesting that if we used up our savings, we would be penniless. Sara and I are fortunate to have regular retirement incomes. Together with our Social Security benefits, our pension checks help pay for our basic living expenses. However, we use our savings to take occasional vacation trips and to otherwise enjoy our retirement. Without any savings to draw upon, our activities would be very limited.

How did I discover that our savings were dwindling rapidly? By using one of those "retirement calculators" that are so popular on the Internet. I went online to the Web site operated by Vanguard mutual funds, www.vanguard.com. I located the company's retirement planning page and found a program that calculates how long your retirement savings will last. (The Vanguard computer program is one of several such programs available from financial service companies. A list is included at the end of the chapter.)

I then entered my financial information, responding to questions that appeared on my screen. When I was finished, I clicked on the "calculate" button, and the machine went to work. It digested my numbers and quickly rendered its verdict. It told me that I would use up all my savings by 2007. That was only eight years away.

The cause of the problem soon became apparent: we were dipping into our savings too often and not earning enough on our investments to replace the money being taken out. And, of course, as our nest egg shrank, the less it earned. Although I didn't like what the computer told me, I was grateful to get the warning in time to do something about it.

The first thing I did was to look at some "what if" calculations. I tried several different scenarios to see what I could do to make our savings last longer. I lowered our monthly expenses and raised the earnings on our investments. That seemed to help. The revised numbers had the effect of stretching out our savings for a few additional years.

But then I realized I had told the computer I would continue to work as a freelance writer until I was 90. On reflection, that seemed to be a bit of a stretch, so I went back and told the computer I would stop earning additional income at age 80. That made the picture worse.

The calculations left me with little choice but to think seriously about how much money Sara and I could save if we trimmed our living expenses. If that's what we have to do in the next few years, we'll do it. But, frankly, it's not a happy prospect.

Making ends meet

To get a fresh perspective on my problem, I chatted with Duane Cabrera, a principal at Vanguard. Cabrera's main goal was to educate retirees and help them to successfully manage their finances throughout retirement.

"There is no magic bullet to keep from running out of money," Cabrera said. "At the end of the day, a retiree's success will be driven by his or her ability to maximize income and minimize expenses."

Cabrera said he has often observed that "retirees have a tendency to understate their expenses and overstate their income." Then, when they are faced with higher-than-expected expenses, they draw out more money from their accounts than is wise. One key to financial success during retirement is to use realistic assumptions about expenses, income, and investment returns when preparing a retirement plan.

Cabrera believes that when people first retire, they should not take out more than 3 to 4 percent of their savings per year. When they get into their seventies, he said, they may be able to increase their withdrawals to 4 to 5 percent. But the key to financial success in retirement is keeping control of one's expenses.

In any event, it seems clear that retirees cannot assume, as many have done in the past, that they will consistently earn 6 to 7 percent on their money. As we saw during 2008 and 2009, a stock market that can rise 20 percent in good years also can fall 30 or 40 percent or more in bad years. Thus, retirees should be prepared to adjust their withdrawals based on market conditions in order to ensure they are not withdrawing too much from their portfolios.

Making your savings last

I wish now that I had run my finances through the Vanguard calculator long before I retired. I would have had a much more realistic idea of how much money we would need to pay our expenses through a 15- to 20-year retirement. I also would have tried harder to improve the returns on our investments.

Until you retire, I discovered, you don't think much about the difference between managing your money in retirement and managing it while you're working. When you're working—and saving for retirement—you pay your bills from your salary or wages. And you try your best to let your savings sit there and grow. But when you retire and you lose your regular paycheck, you are dependent on Social Security and pension checks—if you have a pension—and income from savings. You may also need to work part-time to help out.

If you have maximized your income and minimized your expenses and you still face a gap between what's coming in and what's going out, you will have to see whether it is possible to earn more from your investments. You will have to think carefully about the money in your retirement savings accounts, how that money is invested, what it earns, and how much you can reasonably withdraw each year without seriously reducing the earnings potential of your nest egg. Table 7.1 shows you how long your money will last, depending on the percent you earn each year and the percent you withdraw each year. Plot the number of years remaining by picking your savings growth rate and your rate of withdrawal. (The chart assumes that you are not adding to your savings.) The number at the intersection of these two rates is how many years may be left until your savings are depleted. For example, if your savings grow 3 percent annually and you withdraw your original principal at a rate of 10 percent annually, your savings may last roughly 12 years.

There are three main ways to invest your retirement savings: you can invest for growth, for income, or for a combination of growth and income. This chapter offers some suggestions on how to use your savings to provide a flow of monthly income and some growth as well.

Investing is a highly personal matter involving your financial needs, your time horizon, and your willingness to take risk. That being the case, I believe it's wise for each investor to discuss his or her goals with a financial planner or investment advisor. If you are already retired, an advisor can help you figure out how long your money will last in retirement. If you are still working, an advisor can help you develop an investment plan that will help you reach your goals. Suggestions on how to find a financial planner appear at the end of the chapter.

In the meantime, I am happy to share with you some of the lessons I have learned from my years of investing, watching the market, and making investment mistakes. If you expect to depend on your savings to help support you in retirement, these are lessons you, too, will need to learn. So here they are.

Table 7.1 When Will Your Savings Run Out?

Savings growth rate	\ Withdrawal rate 2%	3%	4%	5%	6%	7%	8%	9%	10%	11%	12%	13%	14%	15%	16%
15%															20
14%														21	16
13%													22	16	14
12%												23	17	14	12
11%											24	18	15	13	11
10%										25	19	15	13	12	10
9%									27	20	16	14	12	11	10
8%								29	21	17	14	12	11	10	9
7%							31	22	18	15	13	11	10	9	9
6%						33	24	19	16	14	12	11	10	9	8
5%					37	26	20	17	14	12	11	10	9	8	8
4%				41	28	22	18	15	13	12	10	9	9	8	7
3%			47	31	23	19	16	14	12	11	10	9	8	8	7
2%		55	35	26	20	17	15	13	11	10	9	8	8	7	7
1%	70	41	29	22	18	15	13	12	11	10	9	8	7	7	6

Withdrawal rate

Source: Oppenheimer Funds, Inc. This chart is intended as educational material about savings and investing and does not predict or depict the rate of return on any mutual fund or other investment. Consult an investment professional for a more specific and detailed analysis of your personal financial situation.

Five golden rules

YOU MUST LEARN HOW TO INVEST

If you are still working and belong to a 401(k) or other company savings plan, you are probably making decisions regarding how to invest your money by choosing from among a small number of investments offered by your company. If you are retired, you still have to make investment choices, but now you can choose from 8,000 mutual funds, at least 8,000 stocks, more than 700 exchange traded funds (ETFs), and countless bonds. And that can be mind boggling.

In either case, if you haven't already done so, it is time to learn how to invest. It is pretty obvious that knowing how to invest is now a required life skill in American society. The ability to save and invest wisely could enable millions of retirees to have a decent lifestyle while they are living into their eighties and beyond. I can foresee the day when the four educational basics will be reading, writing, arithmetic—and investing.

Learning to invest is not difficult. Start with some of the popular investment magazines and TV channels that cover the financial markets on a daily basis. Take a look at some of the many investment Web sites. Dozens of books and videos offer insights into investing. Remember this: before you invest your money, invest your time and learn the basics of investing. It's not hard and it can even be fun. But start now. You owe it to yourself.

THE GREATER THE RISK, THE GREATER THE REWARD

As surely as day follows night, the one rule that never changes on Wall Street is that risk and reward go hand in hand. The greater the risk, the greater the reward, and the greater the reward, the greater the risk. It sounds like a warning you might have gotten from a social studies teacher in high school, but anybody who has been burned in the financial markets knows the old rule is true. You simply can't get huge gains without taking huge risks. And what goes up very fast can also come down very fast, as we learned from two market events of recent memory: the collapse of high-flying Internet stocks during the spring of 2000 and the once-in-a-century stock market crash in 2008–2009, which was caused by a meltdown in the subprime mortgage, banking, and housing sectors. So, when you make any investment, always think about your tolerance for risk versus your desire for safety.

NEVER TRY TO OUTGUESS THE MARKET

Those of us who have been investing for a number of years know the truth of this statement. Remember, in Chapter 5, my tale of losing $70,000 in my 401(k) plan? As I discovered, if you sell everything and get out of the market because you think it is going down, chances are that you will sell at the lowest point and be out of the market when it rebounds. Thus, you will get the losses and miss the gains. Experienced investors know that over the last 83 years, the long-term trend of the market has been up and that if you ignored the short-term gyrations and stayed invested, you would have benefited from those upward movements. Understandably, the financial tsunami in 2008 and 2009 was so traumatic that many investors found it difficult to restrain themselves from selling. But, true to form, after stock prices hit bottom in March 2009, they rebounded strongly in the following months.

GO FOR THE AVERAGES

One of the most tantalizing rules of investing is, "Buy low and sell high." It sounds easy, but it's a very hard thing to do on a consistent basis, as experienced traders will tell you. For investors like you and me, the next best thing is something called "dollar cost averaging." This involves investing the same amount of money in, say, a mutual fund every month over a long period of time. As the price of the fund's shares rise and fall, you will sometimes buy at the highs and sometimes at the lows. But in the long run, you will be buying your shares at an average price, which is a good deal. In any event, it certainly beats trying to decide when the right time is to buy those shares, since you are likely to guess wrong.

SPREAD YOUR RISK

As kids, we learned the old rule, "Don't put all your eggs in one basket." Why? Because if you drop your basket, good-bye eggs. Thus, it makes sense to put your eggs in more than one basket.

That rule has turned out to be good advice for investors, too. People on Wall Street have their own word for it. They call it *diversification.* Decades of experience have shown that your best chance to succeed as an investor is to put portions of your money into several different kinds of investments.

Specifically, diversification involves putting some of your money in stocks, some in bonds, and some in money market funds. Within each category, you also will have a number of choices. For instance, you can invest in stocks of big companies or stocks of small companies, stocks of domestic firms or stocks of foreign firms. As regards bonds, you can choose among government bonds, corporate bonds, municipal bonds, and others. Money market funds vary in their interest rates, but they are basically similar to one another.

The principle of diversification rests on the fact that different types of investments march to the beats of different drummers. When stocks are going up, bonds may be going down, or vice versa. Similarly, when domestic stocks are rising, foreign stocks may be falling. In short, different investments behave differently at different times and, of course, give you different results. By spreading your money around, you can reduce your chances of being hurt financially if one sector of the market should take a big hit. All of that is under what I would consider "normal" market conditions. During the vast sell-off of 2008–2009, market conditions were anything but "normal." In fact, it was one of the few times in market history when diversification did not work because almost everything went down. There was simply no place to hide.

So, even though diversification has a good long-term track record, it is not infallible.

Meanwhile, here's another note of caution about diversification: some investors try to diversify by buying shares in many mutual funds. That may work if the funds have been carefully selected to represent different areas of the investment world, such as large companies, small companies, domestic companies, international companies, and so on. But all too often investors unknowingly buy several funds that all specialize in, say, large-cap value stocks. While the fund names are different, the investment philosophies are the same. Thus, instead of getting diversification, the investor gets a similar result from each of the funds—and more risk than anticipated.

Beyond the golden rules

Once you are comfortable with the idea of diversification, you will want to think about what portions of your money you want to put into stocks, bonds, and money market funds. Here again, Wall Street has an apt phrase. It's called *asset allocation.*

SLICING THE INVESTMENT PIE

There are many ways to slice your investment pie. You can cut it in three pieces—one for stocks, one for bonds, and one for money market funds. You can cut it in half and put 50 percent in stocks and 50 percent in bonds. Or you can put 50 percent in stocks, 40 percent in bonds, and 10 percent in money market funds. You get the idea.

But why does it matter how you allocate your money? Earlier, we talked about diversification and how spreading your money around in different investments was your best protection against the short-term ups and downs of the market. Now, let's look at asset allocation. By my definition, that's a strategy that advises us to lean in the same direction as the market. If stocks appear to be in an uptrend, let's switch some of our bond money to stocks.

Instead of being 50-50 in stocks and bonds, we'll be 80 percent in stocks and 20 percent in bonds.

Professional investors spend a lot of time trying to decide how to allocate their money. If they correctly judge the direction of stocks or bonds, they will do well. And so can you. Becoming an informed investor will help you develop a sense of how the financial markets are moving. And that can help you make intelligent and profitable investment decisions.

Retirees—A special case

For many years, the common wisdom in the investment world was that stocks were suitable for younger investors but not for older investors. The theory was that once you reached retirement age, you had to become more conservative and move your money into bonds and other fixed-income investments, which were judged to be less risky. The thinking was that retirees had to be wary of investing in stocks because, in the event of a market crash, they would lose the savings they needed to live on and might not have time to wait for the market to return to higher ground.

During the decades of the 1980s and 1990s, that view of retirement investing was replaced by another view, which holds that retirees no longer should give up their stocks and move all their money into bonds when they turn 65. In fact, despite the events of 2008–2009, it's still believed that it makes perfect sense for retirees to keep a significant percentage of their money in equities. And here is why.

The longevity case

The Census Bureau tells us that the average 65-year-old can look forward to at least 15 years or more in retirement. Many retirees live into their eighties and even nineties. This is a huge change in life expectancy for most Americans. In 1900, an average 65-year-old had a life expectancy of only a few years. Currently, an average

65-year-old man can expect to live to about age 81. Women can expect to reach about age 84.

If today's retirees have that many years to invest, why shouldn't they take advantage of the higher returns they can get from stocks? The historical record is persuasive: over the 83 years from 1926 through 2008, large-company stocks returned an average of 9.6 percent a year, while long-term government bonds returned 5.7 percent a year, according to Ibbotson Associates, a subsidiary of Morningstar, Inc. By investing in stocks, it would appear, retirees can improve their chances of stretching out their retirement dollars. But be cautious. The long, upward climb in the Ibbotson stock market chart obscures the many market crashes and financial upheavals that have taken their toll on all investors—but especially on people who are preparing to retire.

Indeed, it is worth looking inside the Ibbotson figures at what happened during just the four years between the second and third editions of this book. Between 2004 and 2008, the return for large-company stocks fell from 10.4 percent a year to 9.6 percent a year. That was an 8 percent drop, which reflected the impact of the market turmoil that began in 2007 and carried through 2008 and beyond. At the same time, the return on long-term government bonds rose from 5.4 percent a year to 5.7 percent a year, a 5.5 percent increase. Clearly, in recent years, bonds have done better than stocks.

Inflation is not your friend

Our new and longer investment horizons mean that retirees have to worry more about inflation than they did before. Inflation has always been a concern for individuals who live on fixed incomes, but before the dramatic increase in life expectancy, there may have been less concern about the effects of inflation on retirees. After all, if your retirement was going to last only for a few years, you didn't have to worry much about inflation. But if your retirement is going to last for 15 or 20 years, inflation can have a substantial impact on the value of your savings.

Although inflation has been subdued in recent years, it averaged 2.9 percent a year during the 24 years from 1985 through 2008, according to the folks at T. Rowe Price. For example, if you retired at the beginning of 1985 with $20,000 in savings, the impact of inflation would have reduced your purchasing power to $9,800 by the end of 2008. That's why today's retirees are advised not to be too conservative in their investments. It may seem safe to put all of one's savings in money market funds, bank CDs, or even government bonds, but without long-term growth in your portfolio, your withdrawals can be zapped by inflation.

Your goal as a retiree should be to develop an investment portfolio that provides relative safety, current income for living expenses, and the growth of your savings. How can you do this? The best way is to use a mix of stock, bond, and money market instruments, tailored to your special situation and needs. While stocks suffer from more ups and downs than bonds do, you can reduce the volatility of your stock investments by using conservative mutual funds such as equity income funds, which invest in high-yielding stocks, and balanced funds, which invest in a mix of stocks and bonds. Research by T. Rowe Price shows that in falling markets, these types of funds declined less and came back faster than the overall market.

Our changing financial markets

Financial markets have changed dramatically in the last several decades. Some of these developments have been good for individual investors, others have not. The changes include:

- The creation of the 401(k) plan. This has allowed millions of Americans to save and invest for retirement at the places where they work. This, in turn, has created several generations of new investors whose financial futures depend on the ups and downs of the stock and bond markets.

• The rise of the mutual fund industry. The industry grew during the 1980s and 1990s. Today, there are 8,000 mutual funds holding trillions of dollars belonging to millions of people saving not only for retirement but to buy a house or send their kids to college. The investment companies have created a broad menu of funds that allow individuals to invest across a wide range of industries and countries.

• The emergence of "financial engineering." Now a dominant factor on Wall Street, financial engineering created the ill-fated subprime mortgage derivatives, which destroyed banks, brokerages, and mortgage companies and cost the nation billions of dollars in bailouts. Meanwhile, Wall Street's wizards have developed advanced electronic strategies, which enable them to "flash" trade millions of shares of stocks per second. While this may be good for the professionals, it makes me wonder whether it is futile for me, as an individual investor, to compete in the market against these electronic powerhouses.

• The sleaze on Wall Street. The financial markets have always had their share of scandals and illegal behavior. But the multiple outrages of the last 20 years—from the collapse of Enron to the Ponzi scheme of Bernard Madoff—seem to have marked a new high in bad behavior and a new low in investor confidence in Wall Street and its regulators. For many investors, it may be a long time before they feel they can put their trust in the investment markets.

Turning your nest egg into income

Many retirees, I have found, need to use their savings to produce a monthly income that can help close the gap between their income and their monthly living expenses. The question is, what's the best way to accomplish this goal? I took the question to a friend, Jack R. May, a certified financial planner (CFP) at the firm of Lara, Shull, & May, LLC, in Falls Church, Virginia. I met Jack 25 years ago, when I wanted to develop a better understanding of financial markets, investments, and corporate accounting. At the time, he was teaching financial planning at George Washington University in Washington, D.C. I enrolled in a couple of his courses and learned many valuable things.

I asked Jack what he would recommend to a person who retires at age 66 with Social Security benefits, a company pension, and $100,000 accumulated over many years in a company 401(k) plan. In this scenario, the retiree has rolled over his or her money into a tax-deferred IRA account at a brokerage firm or a mutual fund company. The retiree's basic goal would be twofold: to get as much income as possible and to preserve the nest egg as long as possible by taking only investment income from the $100,000, leaving the principal intact.

One small wrinkle is that at age 70½, as described in Chapter 6, retirees must begin to take money out of their tax-deferred retirement accounts. Of course, there is nothing to prevent a retiree from reinvesting that money in a taxable account. At 70½, the required minimum distribution (RMD) formula requires a roughly 3.65 percent withdrawal to start, but the RMD increases to nearly 5 percent by age 78. Note that required minimum distributions were suspended in 2009 but have resumed in 2010.

One other wrinkle is that many studies have shown that the best way for retirees to make their savings last through retirement is to withdraw no more than 5 percent a year—in this case $5,000. To that, we would add an annual inflation adjustment of 3 percent of the 5 percent—or $150.

So I asked Jack, what would be the best way for a 66-year-old retiree to invest $100,000 to produce a steady flow of monthly income? And what risks would be associated with these investment strategies?

I have asked Jack these questions in the past. But in mid-2009, as this edition was written, Jack's search for income-producing investments was far more difficult because of the historically low interest rate environment created by the Federal Reserve to cope with the 2008–2009 recession. Currently, Jack is looking at yields for three-month Treasury bills and money market accounts that are near zero percent. Rates for CDs are only slightly higher.

Nevertheless, Jack accepted the challenge and suggested five possible investment choices:

1. A laddered portfolio of Treasury bonds and CDs
2. A multisector bond mutual fund
3. A high-quality, balanced mutual fund
4. A variable annuity
5. A managed portfolio of exchange traded funds (ETFs)

In addition, Jack said that before retirees decide where to invest, they must decide how much income they need to generate from their investments. If their portfolios produce more than 5 percent a year, they should leave the remainder invested to help their savings grow.

"The ultimate objective," Jack said, "is not just to provide a required income and preserve your principal today, but to keep pace with inflation." At just 3 percent inflation, he noted, prices will double in 24 years. Although the 2008–2009 market crash left many people wary of stocks, Jack said the best long-run returns have come from stocks. U.S. stocks, he said, offer ownership positions in some of the best companies in the world. Jack thus believes retirees should keep at least a portion of their savings in dividend-paying stocks or dividend-paying mutual funds.

Here are Jack May's five choices for a $100,000 investment that would produce income.

Laddered portfolio of Treasury bonds and CDs

This is the most conservative approach as both Treasury bills/bonds and CDs are government-guaranteed. The purpose of "laddering" the portfolio, Jack said, is to obtain an average of varying interest rates. In addition, with groups of bonds coming due at different times, a chunk of money can become available to the retiree for any special needs without a forced sale of bonds at market prices. In the current era of unusually low interest rates and with most professionals believing that interest rates are likely to rise in the future, a short-to-intermediate time strategy should be considered so as not to lock in low rates for an extended period of time. This way, upon a bond's or CD's maturity, the retiree may be able to reinvest his or her proceeds at higher interest rates.

In mid-2009, as CDs provide higher rates than Treasuries in all current time periods and are insured through the FDIC, they are the better choice for income, Jack said. Since this is not always the case, it is a good idea to compare rates when these investments come due.

To follow this strategy, Jack suggests putting $25,000 each in (1) a six-month CD (at 0.937 percent); (2) a one-year CD (at 1.257 percent); (3) a two-year CD (at 1.686 percent); and (4) a 5-year CD (at 2.449 percent). This will provide only $1,582 annually ($132 a month) at these rates, an average of just 1.58 percent. This approach might be considered if safety rather than income is the top priority.

Multisector bond mutual fund

Bonds are loans typically between governments or corporations and investors. Investors receive interest payments, usually every six months, and their original principal back upon maturity. Mutual fund managers often buy and sell bonds and will have different interest rates and maturities in their funds. A fund's rate, then, is a blend of all the bonds in the portfolio. When bonds are sold initially, they are given credit ratings that reflect the financial soundness of the government agency or business that issues them. The highest rating is AAA. Any bond rated between AAA and BBB is considered an investment grade bond. Anything below BBB is often referred to as a "junk bond."

Not surprisingly, companies with lower credit ratings pay more interest on their bonds than do companies with higher credit ratings. Those higher interest payments are what make junk bonds so attractive to investors. However, investors in high-yield bonds face the "business risk" that a company might not be able to pay the interest on its bonds. The advantage of using mutual funds is that fund managers usually have analysts who review the bonds before they are purchased. Also, the fund managers can get better prices for bonds than individuals can get on their own. In addition, most funds pay out on a monthly basis and thus are ideal for retirement income.

All bond funds are subject to certain risks, especially the movement of interest rates. When interest rates rise, the value of a bond will decline—and vice versa. In 2009, because of an ongoing flight to quality, government bonds rose in price and many were selling at premiums—thus producing historically low yields. At the same time, other nongovernment bonds declined in price and were selling at discounts, thereby producing higher yields.

The primary goal of many bond funds is to produce income. For instance, the Fidelity Strategic Income Fund invests in four bond categories in an effort to provide a relatively stable price with an above-average yield. The fund's mid-2009 allocation was 26 percent in U.S. government bonds; 41 percent in lower-rated, higher-yielding bonds; 15 percent in foreign government bonds; 16 percent in bonds from emerging market countries; and 2 percent in cash. The average credit quality of the portfolio was "A." On September 15, 2009, the Fidelity Strategic Income Fund was yielding 4.49 percent—so, on a $100,000 account, the fund was producing $4,490 a year, or about $374 a month.

If interest rates were to rise, bond prices would fall, but Treasury and corporate bonds often move in different directions so the diversity of the fund would help cushion any loss. Also, the fund managers would be able to add higher-yielding bonds to the portfolio as new money is invested in their fund.

High-quality, balanced mutual fund

Jack said that retirees who are interested in keeping their monthly income flowing also can achieve that goal by investing in a high-quality, balanced stock and bond fund. This approach utilizes the growth and inflation protection potential of stocks and the stability and income of bonds. Further, balanced fund managers realize that many investors buy this type of fund because they are looking for income. By their nature, balanced funds face both interest rate risk and stock market risk, so managers try to invest in a manner that will provide relatively low price volatility and a consistent dividend.

For example, the JP Morgan Investor Balanced Fund is a "fund of funds" (FOF), which invests in 20 other JP Morgan funds. In mid-2009, this fund had an allocation of 54 percent in equities, 45 percent in bonds, and 1 percent in cash. The average credit quality of the bonds was "AA." Its dividend yield on September 15, 2009, was 2.12 percent, paid quarterly. On a $100,000 investment, this would produce an annual income of $2,120 a year, or $530 a quarter.

In a balanced fund, the total return consists of interest from the bonds plus stock dividends and growth from the fund's equities. This should allow a retiree to take a 5 percent annual withdrawal with a 3 percent inflation adjustment.

Variable annuity

Annuities are designed by insurance companies to allow an individual to accumulate a nest egg for retirement, which then can be used to provide a reliable income.

There are two main types of annuities—fixed and variable. Both offer the investor a guaranteed lifetime income but in quite different ways.

A fixed annuity typically converts your investment into a guaranteed income for life. This often provides a high payout because your return comes from both principal and interest.

One objection to fixed annuities is that once you start receiving income, you no longer have access to your investment, and there is no lump sum that could go to heirs. Another objection is that, as life expectancies increase and people live longer, the income does not increase to offset the effects of inflation.

For example, in mid-2009, MetLife was offering a fixed annuity that provided a lifetime income for husband and wife with a yield of about 6.4 percent. On $100,000, the payment was $6,413.95 a year, or $534.50 a month.

Of course, policy payments are eventually dependent on current interest rates. In the past, when interest rates were higher, the lifetime payout for this couple was calculated at $691 a month, or 29 percent higher than today's payout.

Variable annuities, for their part, offer guaranteed lifetime income, periodic payment increases, and death benefits. They are called variable because of the range of investment options available, chiefly in mutual funds. Thus the performance of a variable annuity will be tied to how well its investments perform during the ups and downs of the financial markets.

About a decade ago, variable annuity companies began adding new income-oriented features to make their offerings more attractive for retirement planning.

These features include a system of periodic increases in income. The increases can occur in one of at least three ways. First, most annuities will automatically "lock in" the highest anniversary value of the annuity. This means that the annual payment may start at $5,000 (5 percent of $100,000), but if the portfolio value were to increase to $110,000 the next year, the income would increase to $5,500 for life, even if the portfolio fell back to $100,000 the following year.

Also, some annuities feature an automatic income increase at various age bands. For example, income may start at age 65 at 5 percent of value (say $5,000) and increase to 5.5 percent at age 75, and so on.

Still other annuities provide that the value of a portfolio will be increased by the greater of a fixed percentage, such as 6 percent a year, or the value of the portfolio on its anniversary date. There are likely to be extra charges for these additional features.

One example of the newer type of variable annuity is the Prudential Advanced Series ASAP III, which offers a guaranteed income for the lives of both spouses. Instead of an "annual lock-in" of value, Prudential offers a "daily lock-in," based on the highest value of any day of the year.

In addition, if an individual decides to postpone taking income, the value of the portfolio from which he or she can draw income will increase by at least 6 percent a year.

Finally, an investor could start withdrawing at a 5 percent rate at age 65, and it would automatically increase to 6 percent at age 85. At the death of the first spouse, the remaining investment can be returned to the surviving spouse, or he or she can continue to draw regular payments.

This Prudential annuity charges an annual basic fee of 1.25 percent and an additional fee of 0.95 percent for the income guarantee and other income features. There is an eight-year declining surrender charge, which starts at 7.5 percent.

Anyone considering investing in an annuity should always review the fees and other charges involved. They can take a big bite out of one's portfolio.

MANAGED PORTFOLIO OF EXCHANGE TRADED FUNDS

In the world of investing, one of the most significant innovations in recent years has been the creation of the exchange traded fund, or ETF. The ETF has many features that appeal to investors. It can be bought and sold during the day like a stock and has a low average management fee, generally around 0.25 percent. Since most ETFs are based on stock, bond, commodity, real estate, and other popular indexes, ETFs offer an infinite variety of investment opportunities.

As with stocks and bonds, investors have a choice. They can invest in individual ETFs on their own through their brokers, or they can turn their portfolios over to an ETF fund manager. A growing number of companies now manage money for clients by using ETFs as their investments. The trend, Jack May said, supports the idea that the asset allocation of a portfolio may be more important than specific stocks and bonds.

ETFs give a fund manager the flexibility to underweight or overweight different market sectors and to do so quickly by buying or selling broad index ETFs on the market at any time during the day. In addition, ETF managers are able to take advantage of market trends by using ETFs to invest in real estate investment trusts (REITs), commodities, or the currency exchanges.

One such manager, Sage Advisory Services of Austin, Texas, which has $8 billion under management, oversees a broad group of ETF portfolios. They range from a conservative portfolio with 30 percent stocks and 70 percent bonds to a higher-risk portfolio with 100 percent in stocks.

As of June 30, 2009, the Sage Tactical Moderate ETF portfolio, which aims to be about half in stocks and half in bonds and cash, reported a year-to-date gain of 4.13 percent. On September 15, 2009, it was yielding 3 percent, paying $3,000 a year, or $250 a month. Sage portfolios, it should be noted, are not immune to market fluctuations. In 2008, the Sage Tactical Moderate ETF lost 19.21 percent, although that compared favorably to a general 50-50 stock and bond benchmark, which lost 27.8 percent.

As with the mutual fund strategies, the Sage ETF portfolio's return would be a combination of interest from bond ETFs and dividends and growth from stock ETFs. As with the balanced fund, an investor could withdraw 5 percent a year with an annual inflation adjustment of 3 percent. The annual management fee for this Sage portfolio could be as high as 1.5 percent, depending on the size of the investment.

Summing up

These then are some of the main choices available to investors for drawing income from their savings. If the choices appear weighted toward the conservative side, that seems appropriate during a time when the nation is in a deep recession and the financial markets continue to be volatile.

For more information

Books

Carlson, Robert C., *The New Rules of Retirement: Strategies for a Secure Future*, New York: Wiley, 2004.

Griffith, Bill Jr., *Securing a Retirement Income for Life*, Washington, PA: W.E. Griffith Publications, 2006.

Hebeler, Henry K., *Getting Started on a Financially Secure Retirement*, New York: Wiley, 2007.

Financial Planners

You can get a list of certified financial planners (CFPs) in your community from the Financial Planning Association. Go to their Web site—www.fpanet.org—enter the name of your hometown, and the FPA Web pages will give you the names and phone numbers of financial planners in your area. The FPA's phone number is 1-800-322-4237.

Fee-only planners are represented by the National Association of Personal Financial Advisors. To obtain a list of fee-only planners in your home area, go to the organization's Web site, www.napfa.org, and provide the name and location of your home city. The Web pages will give you a list of fee-only planners in nearby communities. NAPFA's phone number is 847-483-5400.

WEB SITES

Many of the nation's mutual funds operate Web sites that offer advice on investing and retirement. Some sites also have retirement "calculators" that will help you figure out how much you need to save for retirement or how long your money will last in retirement.

Some of the major mutual fund Web sites are found at these addresses:

- American Century Investments: www.americancentury.com
- Fidelity Investments: www.fidelity.com
- MFS Investment Management: www.mfs.com
- Oppenheimer Funds: www.oppenheimerfunds.com
- Putnam Investment Management: www.putnamfunds.com
- T. Rowe Price Associates: www.troweprice.com
- The Vanguard Group: www.vanguard.com

DECISION 8

What should I do about health insurance?

As we journey through retirement, few things are more important to me and to my wife, Sara, than our health insurance. At
our ages, 82 and 80, respectively, we are increasingly vulnerable
to medical problems and the huge expenses that come with
them. Unfortunately, we both know what it's like to need costly
medical attention. Shortly before we retired, I had a quadruple
heart bypass operation, and Sara had surgery for breast cancer.
Fortunately, our company health insurance policies paid for
most of our hospital and doctors' bills. It was a good thing they
did. My medical costs totaled about $45,000, and Sara's were
more than $20,000. Without our insurance, we'd have been in
debt for years.

When Sara and I retired, we lost the health coverage we had at
our companies. So we migrated to Medicare, the federal insurance
program that pays the hospital and doctors' bills of 45 million
elderly and disabled Americans. At the same time, we signed up
for a secondary insurance policy that was offered by GE, Sara's
former employer, as a retirement benefit. The policy, which covers both of us, pays for some of the medical charges not covered by
Medicare. If the GE policy had not been available, we would have
bought a "Medigap" policy.

Why? Basically, because Medicare pays for most, but not all, of
our hospital and doctors' bills. There is literally a gap between
what hospitals and doctors charge us as patients and what
Medicare will pay those providers for their services. Hence, the
name Medigap for insurance policies that help close the gap by
paying for a portion of the bills that Medicare doesn't pay. If we
didn't have this type of coverage, we would have to pay those costs
ourselves, and that could add up to a lot of money over time.

Here's an example of how the Medicare system works when it
comes to doctors' bills: Let's say I go to my doctor and she charges
me $100 for the visit. The doctor sends the bill to Medicare, which
decides that the visit was worth only $80. Thus $80 becomes what
Medicare calls the *approved* charge for that visit. Under federal

rules, Medicare pays only 80 percent of an approved charge. That means that Medicare will pay the doctor 80 percent of $80, or $64. If you have a Medigap policy, it will pay the other 20 percent of the $80, or $16. If you don't have a Medigap policy, you may have to pay the $16 yourself.

That is the way Medicare deals with doctors' bills. But there are many other aspects of Medicare that current and future retirees need to know about. The bottom line is that Medicare is a giant government program and can be complicated and even frustrating at times. However, I will say that Sara and I have been generally satisfied with the way Medicare has handled *our* medical and hospital bills. But if you are a retiree, you can depend on one thing: Medicare will play a major role in the quality and cost of your health care. In order to make the most of Medicare's benefits, you have to understand how the system works.

What is Medicare?

Medicare, run by the Centers for Medicare and Medicaid Services (CMS), is a federal health insurance program for people who are age 65 and older. It also covers people who are under 65 with certain disabilities and people who suffer from what is called end-stage renal disease. The Medicare definition of the latter is "permanent kidney failure treated with dialysis or a transplant."

There are four major parts to the Medicare program.

Medicare Part A

This is the part of Medicare that pays for hospital stays, medical services, home health care, hospice care, and limited care in skilled nursing facilities. Most people do not pay for Part A if they or a spouse have had 40 quarters—equal to 10 years—of Social Security earnings. People with less than 40 quarters may still qualify for Part A but will have to pay a monthly premium. In 2010, people who have 30 to 39 quarters pay $254 a month. With fewer than 30 quarters, the cost is $461 a month.

In 2010, hospital patients pay a $1,100 deductible for each hospital stay of 1 to 60 days. For days 61–90, they pay $275 a day. For days 91–150, they pay $550 a day. Those last 60 days are considered "lifetime" reserve days and can be used only once. Beyond 150 days, the patient pays all costs during a benefit period. A benefit period begins on the day your inpatient stay begins and ends 60 days after your discharge from the hospital or skilled nursing facility.

Medicare Part B

Medicare Part B pays for doctors' bills, medical tests, and medical equipment. For most people, Part B monthly premiums are deducted form their Social Security benefits. In 2010, the Medicare B premium was raised from $96.40 to $110.50. However, because there was no Social Security COLA in 2010, most Medicare enrollees with continue to pay $96.40. High-income enrollees will pay more. In 2010, the premium is $154.70 for individuals with incomes above $85,000 and couples with incomes above $170,000. There are three higher premium levels (see Table 8.1). The 2010 annual Medicare deductible is $155.

While Medicare pays for many hospital and medical services, there are a number of important items that Medicare does not pay for. When my wife and I joined Medicare, we were surprised to discover that it did not pay for dental care, vision exams, eyeglasses (except one pair of glasses or contacts after cataract surgery), and hearing aids.

I wish I had known about the limitations of Medicare before I retired. When Sara and I were working, our company insurance plans covered dental care, routine physicals, and prescription drugs. Once we lost that coverage, we had to pick up those expenses ourselves—and items like gold crowns and hearing aids

Table 8.1   2010 Monthly Premiums for Medicare Part B (Medical Insurance)

If Your Yearly Income Is		
File Individual Tax Return	File Joint Tax Return	You Pay
$85,000 or below	$170,000 or below	$110.50*
$85,001–$107,000	$170,001–$214,000	$154.70*
$107,001–$160,000	$214,001–$320,000	$221.00*
$160,001–$214,000	$320,001–$428,000	$287.30*
above $214,000	above $428,000	$353.60*

*If you pay a late enrollment fee, this amount is higher.
Source: Centers for Medicare and Medicaid Services.

can be quite costly. As a result, our retirement budget should have included a couple of thousand dollars a year for medical, dental, and prescription drug expenses. Keep that in mind when you are drawing up your retirement budget.

Medicare Part C

This is the part of Medicare that allows and even encourages Medicare recipients to get their care from private health plans. For more than a decade, the federal government has supported the creation of Medicare health maintenance organizations (HMOs) and other forms of managed care in the hope of improving the quality of care and saving money. In 1997, Congress made sharp cuts in Medicare spending and created a multilevel managed care program called Medicare + Choice. The program met with only limited success. By 1999, managed care companies began dropping out of the program, complaining that Medicare reimbursements were so low they could not make a profit. By 2005, only 12 percent of Medicare recipients were in HMOs and other managed care plans while 88 percent were in the original Medicare fee-for-service program.

In 2003, when Congress passed the Medicare Prescription Drug, Improvement and Modernization Act (MMA), it changed the name of the Medicare + Choice program to Medicare Advantage. Congress also tried to reawaken the interest of insurers and managed care companies by boosting payments to Medicare health plans by $1.3 billion during 2004 and 2005. The strategy worked. With the extra money, the private health plans reduced premiums and added extra benefits, including vision screening tests, dental care, prescription drugs, and hearing tests. The expanded services attracted many new members. By 2009, some 18 percent of Medicare beneficiaries were enrolled in managed care plans while 82 percent were in what is now called "original Medicare."

Soon after the Medicare Advantage plans got under way, however, the federal generosity to those plans came under criticism because the payments to MA plans were 14 percent higher than the payments made to beneficiaries in original Medicare. In an effort to reduce the disparity, CMS announced that payments to MA plans would be reduced by 4 to 4.5 percent in 2010.

Medicare Advantage

These are the main choices available under the Medicare Advantage program:

MEDICARE HEALTH MAINTENANCE ORGANIZATIONS (HMOs)

If you join an HMO, you will continue to pay Medicare your regular monthly premium. Medicare in turn will pay your HMO a specific sum for your health care, based on geographic and medical considerations. HMOs require their members to use doctors and hospitals in the HMO networks. In many HMOs, your primary-care physician serves as the person who refers you to specialists, and you generally can't see a specialist without a referral. So before you join a Medicare HMO, ask about the HMO's policies regarding referrals and whether the HMO has been sued for refusing to grant referrals. As noted, many HMOs offer hearing, vision, dental, and other benefits not covered by Medicare. Typically, HMOs charge a monthly premium. Charges for office visits and other fees tend to be low, but if you go outside the network, you likely will have to pay the bill yourself. If your HMO has a point-of-service option, it may cover part of out-of-network costs.

Provider-sponsored organizations (PSOs)

A PSO can be created by a group of doctors, hospitals, and other health care providers that agree to give health care to Medicare beneficiaries for a set amount of money from Medicare every month. This type of managed care plan is run by the doctors and providers themselves and not by insurance companies. A PSO resembles a Medicare HMO. Here again, you continue to pay your Part B premium to Medicare, which in turn pays the PSO for your care. Your PSO may charge a monthly premium and per-visit fees. PSOs have been popular in rural areas where there aren't enough people to attract the HMOs sponsored by large insurance companies.

Preferred-provider organizations (PPOs)

A Medicare PPO may have a broader network of doctors and hospitals than an HMO. As in an HMO, however, you pay your Part B premium to Medicare, which then pays the PPO for your care. Unlike HMOs, however, PPOs do not require their members to use the network's providers or to see a primary care physician before going to a specialist. But if you go outside the network, the PPO may pay only part of the bill.

Regional preferred-provider organizations (RPPOs)

The 2003 Medicare Modernization Act called for the creation of 26 Medicare Advantage regions composed of single states or groups of states. Health-care companies were invited to establish PPOs within those regions. The regions were designed to maximize consumer choices, especially in rural areas where Medicare recipients had not had many health-care options, according to the Kaiser Family Foundation. Regional PPOs are required to offer a single Part A/B deductible and a catastrophic cap on out-of-pocket spending. Regional PPOs must also serve at least one entire region and offer the same benefits throughout.

Private fee-for-service plans (PFFSs)

In the last several years, this has been the fastest-growing type of Medicare Advantage plan. To use this plan, you select a private insurance plan that accepts Medicare beneficiaries. You continue to pay your Part B premium. In turn, Medicare pays the private plan for your coverage. Depending on the plan, you are free to go to any doctor or hospital of your choice, or the plan may have a network of providers. The plan may offer benefits not offered by Medicare. But the plan may require you to pay premiums, deductibles, or coinsurance that are different—and sometimes higher—than you would pay in the traditional Medicare program.

Medical savings account plan (MSAs)

Medicare MSA plans have two parts. One is a health plan with a high deductible that may be up to $6,000 a year. Part two is a bank account. Medicare gives your health plan a sum of money each year for your health care. The plan then deposits a portion of this money into your bank account. You may use this money to pay your medical bills during the year. However, you may not contribute personally to your savings account. MSA health plans may provide a network of physicians, but enrollees are not required to use network providers. MSA plans do not provide prescription drugs or a Part D prescription drug benefit.

The amount your health plan puts into your bank account is likely to be less than your deductible. This means that if you use up the funds in your bank account, you will have to pay out of pocket before your insurance coverage begins.

The money you spend for Part A and Part B services will count toward your deductible. Once you have met your plan deductible for the year, your health plan pays 100 percent of your medical expenses. If you have money left in your account at the end of the year, it can remain there and grow tax free.

Special needs plans (SNPs)

SNPs serve people who live in nursing homes or similar institutions or who require nursing care at home. They also serve people eligible for both Medicare and Medicaid or who have specific disabling conditions like diabetes, congestive heart failure, mental health conditions, or HIV/AIDS. An SNP provides case managers to develop a plan of care and to coordinate care for patients. Patients generally have to get their care from doctors and hospitals in the plan's network. SNPs must provide Part D Medicare prescription drug coverage.

These plans are intended to improve care for Medicare and Medicaid beneficiaries with special needs, primarily through improved coordination and continuity of care.

Enrolling, leaving, and changing Medicare plans

People who join a Medicare Advantage plan generally are allowed to change plans only once during the first three months of the year. Special enrollment periods are provided if the plan discontinues serving your geographic area or if you move out of the area served by the plan.

Medicare Part D

In 2006, for the first time in the history of Medicare, millions of beneficiaries were able to get federal financial help for the cost of their prescription drugs. In crafting the new Part D prescription drug law, Congress made fundamental changes in the Medicare program. Instead of letting the Medicare agency run the drug benefit in the way it ran the hospital and medical portions of Medicare, Congress put the new drug benefit in the hands of private health care companies. The companies have considerable flexibility in designing their plans but must adhere to Medicare rules.

Generally, there are two ways for individuals to get financial help with drug bills. Medicare-eligible individuals can enroll in stand-alone prescription drug plans (PDPs) and get all their other medical benefits from original Medicare, or they can enroll in a Medicare Advantage plan, such as an HMO or PPO, where they will get prescription drug coverage plus their regular Medicare benefits.

In October 2009, a Kaiser Family Foundation study, based on CMS data, estimated that in 2010 there will be nearly 27 million Medicare beneficiaries enrolled in Part D, with about 18 million getting their prescriptions from stand-alone drug plans (PDPs) and about 9 million from Medicare Advantage drug plans.

The study estimated that the weighted average monthly PDP premium in 2010 will be $38.85, assuming enrollees remain in their 2009 plans. That is a 10.7 percent increase over the 2009 weighted average monthly premium of $35.09.

Many retirees continue to get their drug coverage through their former employers. The prescription drug law allows those individuals to continue to get drug benefits from their former employers as long as the employers continue their coverage. The prescription drug law provides employers with a 28 percent subsidy for their retiree health expenses as an inducement for them to continue to offer their retiree health plans. The subsidy covers retiree drug costs from $310 to $6,300 per year.

Employers who offer these drug plans generally must notify their retirees by letter if their plans are considered, in an actuarial sense, to be "at least as good" as the basic Medicare drug plan. Retirees should save that letter or document. It will help them prove that they did have equal coverage—or what Medicare calls "credible coverage"—in the event the retiree quits the drug plan or the employer discontinues the coverage.

That's important because if the retiree then applies for drug coverage under a Part D plan, being able to show proof of previous "credible coverage" will help the retiree avoid a late-enrollment penalty.

If a retiree with employer-provided drug coverage does not receive such a letter or document, the retiree should check with the employer's human resources department. Not all drug plans provided by employers will meet the "credible coverage" test.

Choosing a plan

For the majority of people enrolling in Medicare, finding the right prescription drug plan is something of a challenge. It can be a confusing process because in some areas of the country, individuals can choose from more than 40 plans. Fortunately, help is available at www.medicare.gov. Click on "Compare Medicare Prescription Drug Plans." You can do a quick search to find out which plans do business in your zip code, or you can enter the names of specific prescriptions that you take and get more precise information regarding the costs in the plans available to you.

You will find that premiums will vary depending on your zip code and the details of a specific plan, including the amount of the deductible, which cannot exceed $310 in 2010. From plan to plan, the cost of individual drugs will depend on what drugs are available, how they are priced, and the plan's rules concerning use of generics versus brand name drugs.

Part D enrollees face the question of whether the stand-alone prescription drug plans (PDPs) and managed care plans offer the specific drugs that they need. Plans must cover at least two drugs in each therapeutic category of covered Part D drugs, but persons enrolling in drug plans are advised to find out if the drugs they need will be available to them.

Health insurance expert L. Sue Andersen of Silver Spring, Maryland, offers this advice:

The bottom line is, if you do not have a prescription drug plan through a current employment health plan or a retirement health plan, you should sign up for a Part D plan. Even if you don't have high prescription drug costs now, you may have them later, and you may have to pay a penalty to enroll later. If you don't take many prescription drugs, sign up for a plan with a low or zero deductible so you can take full advantage of the $1,890 subsidy provided by Medicare in 2010. If your prescription drug costs exceed the annual limit for your out-of-pocket costs (approximately $4,550 in 2010), you will qualify for catastrophic coverage, which pays most of your drug costs until the end of each year.

As mentioned, individuals who are enrolled in Part D in 2010 pay an estimated average monthly premium of $38.85. Generally speaking, enrollees also pay a $310 deductible in 2010. Enrollment in Part D is voluntary. However, persons who delay enrollment will pay a 1 percent lifetime premium penalty for each month they delay after their enrollment deadline.

Part D enrollees are allowed to change their drug plans each year from October 1 to December 31, to be effective January 1.

Low-income beneficiaries can get "extra help" in paying premiums and deductibles. According to CMS, people were eligible for financial help with Part D expenses if their annual incomes in 2009 were below $16,245 for a single person or $21,855 for a married couple. Slightly higher income levels may apply if you help support relatives who live with you or if you live in Alaska or Hawaii. The limit on financial resources was $12,510 for an individual and $25,010 for a married couple. Resources include savings, stocks and bonds, and real estate other than the value of a person's home. All of these figures may change from year to year.

The Mary Jones story

Let's consider how Part D would work for Mary Jones, who signs up for a stand-alone prescription drug plan (PDP) in 2010. Mary pays an estimated $38.85 monthly premium, or $466.20 a year. When

Mary begins to order drugs under the Part D plan, she pays for the first $310 worth of prescriptions herself; that is her deductible.

After meeting her $310 deductible, Mary begins to get help with her drug expenses. On the next $2,520 worth of drugs, Mary pays 25 percent of the cost, or $630. The government, through her plan, pays the other 75 percent, or $1,890. After that, Mary hits the controversial gap in coverage that is often referred to as the "donut hole." The gap means that Mary must pay the next $3,610 in drug expenses herself. At that point, Mary has paid a $310 deductible, $630 in co-pays, and $3,610 out of pocket, for a total of $4,550. If you add the $1,890 that Medicare paid initially, it means that Mary's drug spending totaled $6,440.

Once Mary spends that amount for her prescriptions, she will have reached the "catastrophic" level, after which Medicare and her plan will pay 95 percent of any additional drug expenses, while she will pay only 5 percent.

Thus there are two ways of looking at Part D and how helpful it is to Medicare recipients. Before Mary reached the $6,440, or "catastrophic," spending level, she spent $4,550, or 70.6 percent of the cost of her prescriptions. If you add the $466.20 yearly cost for her monthly premiums, her total outlay was $5,016.20, or 78 percent of her drug costs. Thus, Part D paid only about 22 percent of her drug costs. On the other hand, if Mary had no other prescription coverage, she would have had to pay 100 percent of the cost herself.

Applying for Medicare

Although I didn't retire and go on Medicare Part B until I was 69, I signed up for Medicare Part A when I turned 65. If you continue to work after you reach 65 and continue to have company health insurance, as I did, you should take Part A at 65 and wait on Part B until you retire. That's fine with the folks at SSA and Medicare, who want people to sign up when they first become eligible. However, as noted, they make exceptions for people who continue to work after 65 or their full retirement age, which is slowly moving up to 67.

If, like many people, you decide to retire when you reach your full retirement age, it's a good idea to sign up for Part A, Part B, and Part D at that time. In fact, notify the SSA three months before you reach that age; that will help ensure that your Medicare coverage will begin when your company insurance is ending.

Don't delay. Delay could cost you money. If you wait 12 months or more to sign up for Medicare, your monthly premiums will go up. Part B premiums will rise 10 percent for each 12 months that you could have enrolled but didn't. The increase in the Part A premium, if you have to pay a premium, will be 10 percent no matter how late you are. To enroll in Medicare, call the SSA number: 1-800-772-1213.

Choosing a Medigap policy

We come now to the ins and outs of choosing a Medigap policy, which, as I've mentioned, is intended to fill the gap between your medical expenses and what Medicare pays. At this point, it won't surprise you to learn that choosing a Medigap policy is a decision that can be rather complicated and requires a careful study of the 11 standard policies that insurers are permitted to sell to consumers after June 1, 2010.

In 2010, both current and future Medigap policyholders will be faced with significant changes in the design and benefits of the standard Medigap policies. Two distinct trends in the Medigap insurance market are reflected in the 2010 offerings. First, there is a greater emphasis on policies that have higher cost-sharing features but have lower premiums. Second, with the advent of the Medicare Part D prescription drug plan, Medigap plans no longer provide drug coverage.

Because the regulation of insurance company products is primarily a state function, the new Medigap menu was drawn up by the National Association of Insurance Commissioners (NAIC) in response to a congressional call for the NAIC to "modernize the Medigap market."

In 1990, after the federal and state governments decided to standardize the various types of Medigap policies, insurance companies were allowed to sell only 10 standard policies, some of which provided coverage for prescription drugs. In the current NAIC redesign, after additions and subtractions, there are 11 benefit packages that insurance companies can offer to consumers (see Table 8.2).

Individuals who hold older policies will be allowed to keep those policies. However, if a current policyholder wants to move to one of the newer policies, he or she will be allowed to do so. It will be up to each insurance company to decide if it wants to require a physical examination. That exam could result in the denial of the application or limits being placed on the coverage of the new policy.

The current Medigap lineup eliminates the old plans E, H, I, and J. Two new plans, M and N, were added for 2010. Plan M provides 50 percent coverage of the Medicare Part A deductible but covers 100 percent of the Part B deductible. Plan N covers the Part A and Part B deductibles but adds a new co-payment structure of $20 for each physician visit and up to $50 for each emergency room visit.

Meanwhile, it is important for consumers to remember that policies in each letter group must offer the same benefits, no matter which insurance company issues the policy. Remember, too, that Medigap policies will pay only for items that Medicare covers. If Medicare won't pay for a medical procedure, neither will a Medigap policy.

Also, bear in mind that not all companies sell all 11 policies, and not all policies are sold in all 50 states. You can only buy a plan that is approved by regulators in your state. And, by the way, it is illegal for an insurance company to sell a Medigap policy to a person who already has one.

Table 8.2 Benefits of Medicare Supplement Plans*

A	B	C	D	F	F†	G	K	L	M	N
Basic, including 100% Part B coinsurance	Basic, including 100% Part B coinsurance	Basic, including 100% Part B coinsurance	Basic, including 100% Part B coinsurance	Basic, including 100% Part B coinsurance	Basic, including 100% Part B coinsurance†	Basic, including 100% Part B coinsurance	Hospitalization and preventive care paid at 100%; other basic benefits paid at 50%	Hospitalization and preventive care paid at 100%; other basic benefits paid at 75%	Basic, including 100% Part B coinsurance	Basic, including 100% Part B coinsurance, except up to $20 copayment for office visit, and up to $50 copayment for ER
	Part A Deductible	Skilled Nursing Facility Coinsurance	Skilled Nursing Facility Coinsurance	Skilled Nursing Facility Coinsurance	Skilled Nursing Facility Coinsurance	Skilled Nursing Facility Coinsurance	50% Skilled Nursing Facility Coinsurance	75% Skilled Nursing Facility Coinsurance	Skilled Nursing Facility Coinsurance	Skilled Nursing Facility Coinsurance
		Part A Deductible	Part A Deductible	Part A Deductible	Part A Deductible	Part A Deductible	50% Part A Deductible	75% Part A Deductible	50% Part A Deductible	Part A Deductible
		Part B Deductible		Part B Deductible	Part B Deductible					
				Part B Excess (100%)	Part B Excess (100%)	Part B Excess (100%)				
		Foreign Travel Emergency	Foreign Travel Emergency	Foreign Travel Emergency	Foreign Travel Emergency	Foreign Travel Emergency			Foreign Travel Emergency	Foreign Travel Emergency

Table 8.2 Benefits of Medicare Supplement Plans* (continued)

A	B	C	D	F	F†	G	K	L	M	N
							Out-of-pocket limit $[4,620] paid at 100% after limit reached	Out-of-pocket limit $[2,310] paid at 100% after limit reached		

*For effective dates on or after June 1, 2010.

†Plan F also has an option called a high deductible plan F. This high deductible plan pays the same benefits as Plan F after one has paid a calendar year [$1900] deductible. Benefits from high deductible plan F will not begin until out-of-pocket expenses exceed [$1900]. Out-of-pocket expenses for this deductible are expenses that would ordinarily be paid by the policy. These expenses include the Medicare deductibles for Part A and Part B, but do not include the plan's separate foreign travel emergency deductible.

Source: National Association of Insurance Commissioners.

When shopping for Medigap insurance, it is important to compare premiums because there are great variations in the amounts that different companies charge for the same coverage. In evaluating premiums, be sure you are comparing identical plans. One key to price shopping is to understand that companies use three different methods to calculate annual premiums.

ISSUE AGE

The premium is set when you buy the policy. You continue to pay the premium required of a person of the same age you were when the policy was issued. For example, if you buy a policy at age 65, you will always pay the rate the company charges people who are 65, regardless of your advancing age. However, the rate for 65-year-olds could go up.

ATTAINED AGE

The premium is based upon your current age and increases automatically as you grow older. Typically, these plans will appear to be less expensive at younger ages, but they may cost considerably more in later years. The vast majority of policies sold in this country are based on attained age.

NO AGE RATING

A few companies charge the same premium for all policyholders regardless of age. These policies may be more expensive initially but less expensive in the long run. For people over age 75, a policy with no age rating may be less costly than one based on attained age. You should compare policies based on what they are likely to cost you over the next 5 or 10 years. Be alert for discounts that some policies make available to couples or nonsmokers.

CAN YOUR MEDIGAP APPLICATION BE TURNED DOWN?

One of the most important things for future retirees to know is that there is a one-time open-enrollment period for buying Medigap insurance. If you apply for a Medigap policy within six months of signing up for Part B, you cannot be turned down, according to health insurance expert L. Sue Andersen. However, after the six-month period, the company may ask you to fill out an application that asks questions about your health. This is called "medical underwriting."

If you have a medical condition, said Andersen, the insurance company may deny your application or may accept your application but refuse to cover your "preexisting" medical condition for a period of up to six months. Under current law, Andersen noted, if an insurance company imposes such a waiting period, it must reduce the period by one month for each month you had other health insurance before your application. If you had more than six months of prior coverage, the Medigap health plan cannot refuse to cover your preexisting condition.

For people who work after age 65 and for younger people who receive Medicare, there are special open-enrollment rules.

What does Medigap cost?

When it comes to Medigap policies, it pays to shop around. Prices vary widely for policies that provide the same coverage. So where can you get a list of insurance companies that sell Medigap policies and the prices of those policies?

A good place to start is with the state insurance department in the state where you live. An insurance company cannot sell you a Medigap policy unless it has been approved for sale in your state. Thus, state insurance departments are likely to be able to provide you with information about companies that sell Medigap policies in your state and about the prices of those policies.

The Maryland Insurance Administration, for instance, has a list of companies that sell Medigap policies in the state and the prices they charge. The 2009 list shows that for 65-year-olds, Plan A policies sold for as little as $836 and as much as $2,541 a year. Plan F policies sold as low as $1,373 and as high as $3,972 a year.

Nationally, prices vary from state to state, and, as mentioned, not all companies sell all policies in all states. A 2009 national survey by TheStreet.com Ratings, Inc., of Jupiter, Florida, showed that Plan A policies for a 70-year-old female sold for as little as $423 and as much as $5,909. For Plan F policies, the lowest price was $587, and the highest was $9,021. Given these wide variations in price, it is obviously important to shop around and carefully compare the cost of Medigap policies that are available in your state.

Returning to Medigap

People who join Medicare HMOs and other Medicare Advantage plans do not need Medigap policies. But once you give up your policy, it may be difficult to get it back. Or, if you can get new Medigap coverage, it may not be the policy you want. However, Medicare points out that there are at least three limited situations in which people who have joined Medicare HMOs may be able to get new Medigap policies or retrieve the ones they had before they joined a managed care plan:

- You can get your Medigap policy back if you lost your health coverage through no fault of your own, as when your HMO quit the business.
- You can get your policy back if you joined an HMO for the first time but decided to leave within a year.
- If you were new to Medicare when you joined an HMO and thus did not have a Medigap policy, you can probably get any policy you want if you decide to leave the HMO within a year.
- If you had a retirement health plan that ended, you may get a Medigap plan or join a Medicare Advantage plan.

To get those protections, you have to apply for a Medigap policy within 63 calendar days after your previous coverage ends. To see how the rules may apply to you, call 1-800-633-4227 and talk to a Medicare customer service representative.

For more information

WEB SITE

The official Medicare Web site, www.medicare.gov, contains basic information about Medicare and its many features. It allows you to compare health insurance policies and nursing homes. You can also read, print, and order booklets published by the Centers for Medicare and Medicaid Services.

TELEPHONE NUMBERS

Call 1-800-MEDICARE (1-800-633-4227) for information and publications. TTY users should call 1-877-486-2048.

PUBLICATIONS

Medicare publishes dozens of helpful booklets, including:

- *Medicare & You 2010* (CMS Pub. 10050)
- *Choosing a Medigap Policy: A Guide to Health Insurance for People with Medicare* (CMS Pub. 02110)
- *Medicare Basics: A Guide for Families and Friends of People with Medicare* (CMS Pub. 11034)
- *Your Guide to Medicare Prescription Drug Coverage* (CMS Pub. 11109)
- *Guide to Choosing a Nursing Home* (CMS Pub. 02174)
- *Medicare and Home Health Care* (CMS Pub. 10969)

Consumer Health information Web sites:

- Medicare Rights Center. www.medicarerights.org
- Kaiser Family Foundation. www.kff.org
- National Council on Aging. www.ncoa.org

What should I do to prepare for serious illness?

I don't know what scares you about growing older, but I can tell you what scares me. It's the idea that my health or the health of my wife, Sara, might deteriorate to the point where one of us would have to become a resident of a nursing home for an extended period of time. What frightens me isn't just the prospect of illness and the regimentation of nursing home life but the very real threat that we could be wiped out financially by the cost of that care.

The national average fee for a private room in a nursing home is $219 a day, or a whopping $79,935 a year, according to a 2009 survey by the MetLife Mature Market Institute. In the Washington, D.C., area where I live, private rooms cost an average of $285 a day, or $104,025 a year, according to MetLife. At those prices, most of the people I know wouldn't be able to pay for nursing home care for very long. I know we wouldn't.

But what happens if you are so ill you have to stay in a nursing home indefinitely? It's no secret. Inevitably, you go on Medicaid, a medical program for the poor, which allows you to remain in a nursing home without paying. But to become eligible for Medicaid, you have to pay the nursing home until you virtually run out of money.

That unhappy prospect led Sara and me to sign up for long-term-care insurance, also called nursing home insurance, when the *Washington Post* offered it to its employees and spouses a few years ago. The group policy was issued by CNA Insurance. In retirement, I continue to pay for our policies. Naturally, I hope we will never have a reason to use them. When we bought the policies, we were hoping that if we ever had to live in a nursing home, the insurance payments would ease the bite of the nursing home bills, protect us from being wiped out financially, and keep us off the Medicaid rolls. We still feel that way.

Buying a long-term-care policy

The group policy that Sara and I bought from CNA through the *Post* originally paid $110 a day for nursing home care and $55 a day for home care, with a maximum total benefit of $220,000 each, which equates to 5.5 years in a nursing home. My policy, which I took out at the age of 64, costs $1,089.48 a year. Sara's policy, which she took out at the age of 62, originally cost $945.96 a year but now costs $1,724.36 because her benefits were recently upgraded to $130 a day for nursing home care and $65 a day for home care. Her maximum total benefit rose to $260,000.

Thus, our annual long-term-care bill is now $2,813.84. That may seem like a lot of money, but the fact is that the yearly bill for our group policy is relatively cheap when you look at the price of many individual policies being sold today.

Buying a long-term-care policy is a lot like buying a car. The more bells and whistles you want, the more it costs. You can get a policy that pays $100, $150, or even $200 a day for nursing home care. As the benefits go up, so does the cost of the policy.

Frankly, I didn't do a lot of research on the *Post*'s CNA policy when I bought it 18 years ago. I wish I had. I might have shopped around for an individual policy that would have given Sara and me more financial protection than we get from the *Post*'s group policy, although it probably would have cost us much more money. If you're interested in long-term care, remember that the younger you are when you buy a policy, the less it will cost per year.

After I retired, I did some research on long-term-care policies. The more I look at the provisions of my policy, the more things there are that I wish I could change. For instance, we do not have inflation protection. Without it, we will still be getting a daily benefit of $110 to $130 when nursing homes in the Washington area cost an average of $271 a day.

There are other aspects of our policies that I dislike, including the following.

The waiting period

The policy has a 60-day waiting period for nursing home benefits and a 15-day wait for home care benefits. That means that if I have to go to a nursing home, I would have to pay for the first 60 days myself. At an average of $271 a day, that would be $16,260. That's a pretty big deductible.

Waiving the premium

The insurance company says that if I go to a nursing home, I can stop paying the premiums on my long-term-care policy. That sounds generous, but wait—that benefit also doesn't kick in until I've been in a nursing home for 60 days. So I'm spending $16,260 and still paying my premiums during those 60 days.

Getting paid

To collect under my policy, I would need to show that I have a "qualifying impairment," meaning that I am unable to perform by myself at least two of the so-called activities of daily living. These activities include eating, dressing, going to the toilet, bathing, moving from the bed to the chair, and managing medications.

Who decides whether I can or can't do these things? The insurance company, of course. The policy says that the company will consult with my doctors and caregivers, but it's free to have its own doctor examine me to see whether I have a "qualifying impairment."

Higher rates

The policy says the company can't raise my individual premium, but it can raise the rate of everybody in my class—that is to say, everybody who is my age and who bought the same policy when I did years ago. Thus far, our rates have stayed about the same. But rates do go up from time to time at various companies. And I'm not sure how much more I am prepared to pay.

One other thing that our policy lacks is any sort of "nonforfeiture" clause. The clause comes into effect if you stop paying your premiums after paying them for a specified number of years. It assures you that you will still receive a portion of your long-term-care benefits.

While my CNA policy has the aforementioned negatives, it also has some relatively attractive features, including the following.

Home health care

The insurer will pay for home health-care services from a variety of therapists, registered or licensed nurses, home health-care aides, or medical social workers. Better yet, the insurer also will pay for "homemaker services, such as cooking, cleaning, laundering, organizing bills for payment, and running errands." There is, however, one small catch: a person you hire to provide home health-care services must be a registered or licensed nurse or an aide who works for an organization that is licensed, registered, or accredited by either state or professional organizations.

Alternate plan of care

My policy provides that, if I need them, the company will pay for special treatments and devices if the doctors and the insurer agree that they would be medically beneficial.

What do long-term-care policies cost?

The cost of a long-term-care policy depends on several factors: your age, your health, where you live, and the features included in the policy. But, in a larger sense, the price you pay also will reflect the high cost of long-term care in the United States.

These costs are particularly evident at the nation's nursing homes. As mentioned, in 2009, a private room cost an average of $219 a day, or $79,935 a year, according to a survey by the MetLife Mature Market Institute. A semiprivate room cost $198 a day, or

$72,270 a year. This may not include additional expenses incurred by residents, such as managing medications.

Assisted-living facilities also are quite costly. In 2009, the national average monthly rate was $3,131, or $37,572 a year, according to MetLife. Again, this may not include additional expenses incurred by residents.

MetLife studies also found that, in 2009, it cost $21 an hour to hire home health aides provided by a home care agency. An eight-hour shift thus would cost $168, or $1,176 for a seven-day week.

Interestingly, statistics show that only about 20 percent of people who need long-term care are residents of nursing homes. The other 80 percent live at home or in assisted-living facilities.

Given the cost of long-term care, it is no surprise that the prices of new long-term-care insurance policies have been on the rise. It is also no surprise that many individuals have bought insurance to protect their savings.

To get a realistic look at the costs of long-term-care policies, I talked with Arthur Stein, a certified financial planner in Bethesda, Maryland. Stein has sold long-term-care insurance for 14 years.

Stein showed me the cost estimates and other details of policies issued by three insurance companies: John Hancock Life Insurance, Prudential Insurance, and Genworth Financial (a spin-off from General Electric). Stein and I looked at the prices for couples at two age levels: 65 years of age and 52 years of age.

The monthly premiums for Mr. and Mrs. Older Couple were John Hancock, $527; Prudential, $505; and Genworth, $437.

The monthly premiums for Mr. and Mrs. Younger Couple were John Hancock, $314; Prudential, $288; Genworth, $258.

These policies include a 20 to 40 percent discount for couples when compared to the rates for single individuals. They do not include preferred health discounts.

What would the couples get for their money if they were to buy these policies?

For each spouse, the policies would provide the following: $150 per day for care in nursing homes or assisted-living facilities and $150 a day for home care. The policies would pay for four years—the equivalent of $219,000—but would allow each spouse to share as needed from their pool of eight years of coverage.

The policy also would provide inflation protection at a rate of 5 percent compounded annually, meaning that the initial $150-a-day coverage would rise by 5 percent each year without any increase in premium. Each policy includes a 90-day waiting period for benefits.

All three companies allow policyholders to stop paying their premiums when their waiting period ends and they begin receiving benefits.

In order to receive their daily benefit, policyholders would have to be unable to perform two out of six activities of daily living (ADLs) or suffer from cognitive impairment.

While physical exams generally are not required to be approved for a policy, Stein said, an insurance company would want to see the results of a physical before paying benefits.

All three policies also would provide home care help from health aides and other caregivers.

Stein noted that, before buying a policy, individuals should ask about a company's financial ratings from national rating agencies. A company's ability to pay claims—not only at the present time but years into the future—is an important factor for consumers to consider when shopping for a policy.

The three policies that Stein discussed all include a "contingent nonforfeiture" feature. This means, Stein said, that if a company raises the cost of a policy and the policyholder is unable to pay the increase, the policyholder can reduce his or her benefit so the savings approximately equal the amount of the cost increase.

This goes part of the way toward addressing what I see as one of the discouraging features of long-term-care insurance: that people can pay their premiums for many years but if they stop paying because the company raises its rates, or for any other reason, their policy lapses and they lose everything they have paid over the years.

It can be argued, of course, that long-term-care insurance is really no different than auto, fire, or disability insurance. When you stop paying on those policies, you also lose your coverage. But it seems to me that long-term-care insurance should be in a separate category, given the near-certainty that an individual will need his benefits eventually.

In any event, many more individuals might be willing to buy long-term-care insurance if they could expect some return of their money when they can no longer afford the premiums.

I also believe that sales of long-term-care insurance in this country would be encouraged if insurance companies could find a way to turn these policies into savings vehicles—especially for those who pay for 25 or 30 years and never use the benefits.

Who needs long-term-care insurance?

That brings us to a basic question about long-term-care insurance: how do you decide whether to buy a policy? The answer, I find, depends on your financial and family situations.

Let's talk first about your family situation. If you become seriously ill and have a spouse or child who would be willing or able to be an active caregiver, you may have a good chance to remain at home instead of going to a nursing home. Thus, you may not need nursing home benefits, although a policy providing home health benefits might be useful. However, there is no guarantee that your spouse or children, devoted as they might be, could care for you for very long. When people develop Alzheimer's disease or other serious medical problems, there may be no choice but to seek the 24-hour care available in a nursing home.

What about the financial issues? Leta S. Blank, coordinator for the Senior Health Insurance Assistance Program (SHIP) in Montgomery County, Maryland, says individuals should buy a long-term-care policy only if their annual retirement incomes are over $50,000 and if they have assets of $100,000 to $500,000, not including their home or car. Blank also warns, "Buy long-term-care insurance only if you can afford it without making a lifestyle change and if you have the ability to afford a 20 percent to 50 percent increase in premiums in future years."

But what are the chances that you will ever go to a nursing home, or, if you do enter a nursing home, that you will spend much time there? According to AARP, research suggests that about half of today's older people will spend some time in a nursing home—from as little as a few weeks to as much as five years. AARP cites several factors that could increase your chances of going to a nursing home:

- You live alone or have no relatives who could care for you at home.
- Your family members tend to live into their eighties or older.
- Your family has a history of heart problems, high blood pressure, diabetes, or some other serious or chronic health problems.
- Your family has a history of stroke or Alzheimer's or Parkinson's disease.

If, after considering all these factors, you decide to buy a long-term-care policy, be prepared to do some hard work to get the right policy from the right company. You'll certainly need to shop around, which means interviewing salespeople from several companies and being steadfast in your refusal to sign anything until you've completed your comparisons. Do not buy any policy that you don't completely understand. People who buy policies get a 30-day "free look" during which they can return the policy and get a refund.

Beyond the nursing home: other options

Until a few years ago, the nursing home was about the only place in town where you could place an elderly parent or spouse who was no longer physically or mentally able to live in his or her own home. That situation has changed dramatically. Today, in most areas of the country, there are many more options, including group homes, assisted-living facilities, and continuing-care retirement communities. The growth of these facilities has been prompted by the recognition by both nonprofit organizations and entrepreneurs that there is a serious and growing demand for services for the elderly. In addition, many people reaching their sixties and seventies want to prepare for the day when they can no longer live independently.

It is also clear that not all elderly people need a nursing home with its skilled 24-hour care or even its long-term custodial care. Instead, many people can get by with help just in preparing meals, dressing, bathing, or some of the other activities of daily living. American entrepreneurs, always quick to spot a business opportunity, foresaw that as the U.S. population grew older, millions of elderly persons would need that kind of help. Thus was born a new assisted-living industry. Currently, about one million Americans live in more than 36,000 assisted-living facilities, according to the Assisted Living Federation of America.

The trend also has resulted in the creation of thousands of continuing-care retirement communities—often called CCRCs—where you can move in while you are still in good health, and later, if your health deteriorates, you can move to higher levels of care until, finally, you reach the nursing home level. One word of caution about CCRCs, though: be prepared for a case of "sticker shock" when you see the cost of some of these facilities.

If Sara or I became ill, we would first try to care for each other at home if possible. But as I said before, we would not expect our children to be caregivers. They have their own homes, families, and busy, demanding jobs. While they would be sympathetic and helpful, we'd prefer to organize our own care.

If necessary, we'd hire a home health care aide. Charges vary around the country, but in the Washington, D.C., area, home health agencies charge an average of $15 to $18 an hour, according to area agencies. Charges depend on the number of hours worked and whether evenings, weekends, or holidays are involved. Agencies generally have a four-hour minimum.

For these expenses, we would get some help from our *Washington Post* CNA long-term-care insurance policy, which would pay $55 to $70 a day for home care, or somewhat less than half the cost for an eight-hour shift. But if home care didn't meet our needs, we might decide to go to an assisted-living residence. These establishments are intended for people who can't live on their own but don't require 24-hour skilled nursing care either.

Finding the right assisted-living residence at the right price can be difficult. Nationally, large facilities cost an average of $3,000 a month plus entry fees. Smaller group homes may cost $2,000 to $2,500 a month but may lack some of the amenities or services of the larger homes, such as a full-time staff member for activities.

I talked with Karen Love, founder and board chair of the Consumer Consortium on Assisted Living, about the growth and challenges facing the assisted-living industry. "The assisted-living industry has grown phenomenally in the past two decades," she told me. "There are approximately one million residents living in assisted living. Compare this to the estimated 1.6 million nursing home residents, an industry that has been around significantly longer than assisted living, and one understands the explosive growth experienced in assisted living." Current economic conditions, she noted, have slowed the growth and development of assisted-living residences, but she expects the industry to hold steady for the next two years.

"There are a number of significant challenges facing assisted living: developing more options to make assisted living available to low-to-moderate income individuals; ensuring that person-centered care, seen as the gold standard, is the norm; and addressing the direct care workforce crisis." While baby boomers have been the driving force behind finding alternative means of long-term care other than nursing homes, Love added, "They will also be a driving force behind reshaping quality care and services to support the often physically frail and cognitively impaired resident population of assisted living."

The continuing-care option

Perhaps the most attractive option at our stage of life is a continuing-care retirement community, called a CCRC for short. A CCRC provides both housing and access to health care at three levels:

- Independent living. You live in your own cottage or apartment for as long as you are physically and mentally able to.
- Assisted living. If, as time passes, you require help with dressing, bathing, eating, or any other activities, you can move to the assisted-living area or receive the services you need in your home.
- Skilled nursing care. If you require skilled nursing care, you can move to a residence that provides specific care, which is part of your CCRC.

To get a sense of what a CCRC is like, Sara and I visited the pastoral 130-acre Asbury Methodist Village in Gaithersburg, Maryland. I also talked with Douglas W. Leidig, chief operating officer of Asbury Communities, Inc.

Asbury Communities, a nonprofit corporation, supports several not-for-profit continuing-care retirement communities: the Asbury Methodist Village campus in Gaithersburg, Asbury-Solomons Island in Solomons, Maryland; Bethany Village in Mechanicsburg, Pennsylvania; Epworth Manor in Tyrone, Pennsylvania; Invernesss Village in Tulsa, Oklahoma; and Springhill in Erie, Pennsylvania. It also supports the Asbury Foundation, a 501(c)(3) organization that secures support to enhance the quality of life for seniors served by the Asbury system of communities.

Asbury Methodist Village, founded in 1926 as a home for retired Methodists, has grown into a community with more than 1,300 residents. Asbury is open to all, regardless of sex, creed, color, religion, or national origin.

Like many CCRCs, Asbury offers its residents a sense of security because they know that if they become ill temporarily or need long-term care as they age, it will be available in familiar surroundings. Asbury managers, moreover, provide residents with opportunities for an active physical and intellectual life. Residents can take part in a variety of programs and use the community's recreational facilities. Sara and I liked the CCRC concept and were favorably impressed by the caring attitude we saw at Asbury.

Asbury and most other CCRCs require both entry fees and monthly fees. If we wanted to move to Asbury, the managers would study our financial assets and monthly incomes to see whether we could afford to live there for an extended period of time. Our costs would depend largely on the kind of housing we selected. To move there, we'd first have to sign a contract that spells out the details of what we'd pay and what we'd get in return. The contract also would tell us what additional costs to expect if we had to move to assisted living or to the nursing home.

Retired couples often come to Asbury after selling their homes and using the proceeds to pay the entrance fee for a single-family villa or an apartment. The 2009 standard entrance fee for a villa ranged from $390,000 to $480,000. For an apartment, the 2009 entry fee ranged from $58,000 to $451,900. Residents of villas paid a 2009 monthly fee of $1,555 to $1,635. In the apartments, singles paid a 2009 monthly fee of $1,423 to $3,164, depending on the size of the apartment. There is an extra $613 monthly charge for a couple.

In addition to the villas and apartments, there are other apartments—called Kindley at Asbury Methodist Village—for people who need assisted living.

There are no entry fees for persons who enter Asbury from the outside community and go directly into assisted living. However, the monthly fees are 5 to 17 percent higher than for those who move from independent living to assisted living. Monthly fees in assisted living are tied to the level of care required, of which there are three. The 2009 monthly fee in Kindley at Asbury Methodist Village for persons who enter from the outside community—for level one care—was $5,962 for a single person. At level three, the monthly fee rose to $8,669 for a single person. Couples paid a higher rate.

The villa or apartment entrance fee does not offer any equity ownership in a villa or apartment. However, it is possible to get a refund of one's entrance fee under certain circumstances. An incoming resident has three choices: the standard entrance fee plan, a 90 percent refundable plan, and a 100 percent refundable plan. These latter two plans are priced above the standard entrance fee plan. No interest is paid on any plan.

As of 2009, more than 60 percent of new residents chose the standard entry fee plan; the other residents were typically split between the 90 and 100 percent refund plan options.

Asbury officials point out that their financial structure has many benefits. "Although you are paying a significant sum as a 'down payment' up front, the monthly fees throughout the remainder of one's time at the community are significantly lower than they otherwise would be for a comparable rental property, especially when you take into account all the benefits and services that are included," one said.

"In addition, in a 'down economy' such as we have encountered post-2008, the buying power of community living is a welcome 'economy of scale' that helps individuals to fight inflation and realize additional value for their retirement dollar."

"Finally," the officials said, "Asbury provides a 'care assurance' benefit, which means that even if residents outlive their financial resources (through no fault of their own), Asbury's Foundation raises funds to pick up the financial slack, and residents have never been asked to leave the community for their inability to pay the monthly fees."

Asbury is one of many CCRCs in the Washington area. Each one is different. Housing, recreation facilities, entrance fees, monthly charges, and contracts all vary. People in the CCRC business like to say, "When you've seen one CCRC, you've seen one CCRC."

If you're interested in a CCRC, the best advice is shop around. If you want to move into a CCRC, consult a lawyer before signing any contract.

CCRC contracts generally fall into three categories, all of which include housing and residential services but differ in the amount of health care they cover and in how you pay for accommodations, services, and health care. Here are some definitions:

- The "extensive" or "A-type" contract provides for the prepayment of health-care expenses in a manner similar to an insurance arrangement; it is sometimes known as a "life care agreement." Extensive agreements offer the most health-related services for one predetermined monthly fee, which does not change with an increase in the level of care received by the resident.

- The "modified" or "B-type" contract includes a specified amount of long-term health care in the monthly fee. Additional health care beyond the prepaid amount is available on a fee-for-service basis.

- The "fee-for-service" or "C-type" contract does not include long-term health care in its monthly fee. While residents receive priority admission to the assisted-living and skilled-nursing-care facilities, they pay the full daily rate for the applicable level of care.

Asbury Methodist Village is a C-type, or fee-for-service, organization. If Sara and I were residents of Asbury and had to receive skilled nursing care, it would cost from $284 to $359 a day, depending on the level of care. However, our long-term-care policy would pay only $110 a day for me and $140 a day for Sara. If and when we ran out of money, we probably would be eligible for the Maryland Medicaid program, which covers the cost of room and board and skilled nursing care services. Items such as private duty nurses, hair appointments, and so on, are not included as Medicaid-covered expenses. In the Asbury system, 32 percent of nursing home residents are on Medicaid.

The Asbury Foundation annually provides funding support for benevolent care and other capital and special programs. More than $3.7 million in new gifts and pledges were contributed to the Asbury Foundation in 2008. Across the Asbury system of communities, more than $1.7 million in benevolent care assistance helped 51 independent-living and assisted-living residents who had outlived their resources. In addition, Asbury provided $4.6 million in uncompensated services to those residents on Medicaid.

That generosity is in keeping with the long-established tradition at Asbury that the organization does not ask residents to leave because they cannot afford to stay there, said Douglas W. Leidig, Asbury's chief operating officer.

The financial reality of operating Asbury, Leidig noted, is that the organization's income from monthly fees doesn't always cover its expenses. What keeps Asbury going, he said, are the entrance fees, the ability to invest that money, and the charitable donations that the Foundation receives. The income earned from investments and the donations for care assurance help cover operating expenses.

It all makes sense, of course. But it also makes me wish we had saved more money during our working years. One of these days, we may need it.

For more information

The following organizations can provide information on home care, assisted-living facilities, small group homes, nursing homes, and continuing-care retirement communities:

- Consumers interested in learning more about CCRCs can contact the Commission on Accreditation of Rehabilitation Facilities (CARF)/Continuing Care Accreditation Commission (CCAC). CARF-CCAC is the major accrediting body for CCRCs in the United States. Phone: 1-866-888-1122. Their Web site, www.carf.org, offers a consumer guide to CCRCs.

- The Assisted Living Federation of America (703-894-1805) offers a free package of consumer information, including the *Guide to Choosing an Assisted Living Residence*. The group's Web site is www.alfa.org.

- The National Association for Home Care and Hospice offers an online guide to choosing a home care provider, as well as other consumer information. The Web site is www.nahc.org.

- The American Health Care Association represents long-term-care and assisted-living providers. For free information on long-term health-care options, call 202-842-4444. The group's Web site is www.ahca.org.

- The Consumer Consortium on Assisted Living (CCAL) publishes a booklet titled *Choosing an Assisted Living Facility: Considerations for Making the Right Decision*. The booklet costs $12.95. A purchase form is available at CCAL's Web site, www.ccal.org. To order by phone, call 703-533-8121.

- The National Association of Professional Geriatric Care Managers helps families coordinate care for parents or spouses who need medical treatment or assistance with daily tasks. Fees vary. The organization's Web site is www.caremanager.org. For information, call 520-881-8008.

A number of organizations provide information on long-term-care insurance and suggestions on how to shop for policies:

- The State Health Insurance Assistance Program (SHIP) has counselors in many communities across the country who can offer advice on Medicare, Medicaid, Medigap, and long-term-care insurance. Phone numbers of local counselors are listed in the back of the booklet *Medicare and You 2009/2010*, which is sent to most Medicare recipients. The information also is available at www.medicare.gov.

- The General Services Administration's Federal Consumer Information Center publishes a free *Guide to Long-Term Care Insurance* prepared by America's Health Insurance Plans (AHIP). The guide is available at www.pueblo.gsa.gov or by phone: 1-888-8 PUEBLO.

DECISION 10

Where do I want to live after I retire?

The question of where to live after you retire can have a certain "Fantasy Island" quality. It's easy to imagine yourself retiring and moving to that fabulous vacation spot where you spent two weeks soaking up the sun and scuba diving. Wouldn't it be great fun to live there full-time?

Or perhaps you can see yourself moving to that great little town in the West where you went to college. If you lived there, you could wake up in the morning and look at the mountains where you love to hike. And you could take some of those history courses you didn't have time for when you were in school. What a pleasant life that would be!

Over the years, Sara and I have watched many of our friends and relatives pursue their retirement dreams by packing up and moving to places where they found a better climate, a more interesting lifestyle, or a lower cost of living. Often, I've noticed, retirement moves are determined by the whereabouts of family members. Many of the people who live in our retirement community came here from distant places because they have children and grandchildren who live nearby. They moved to be closer to them.

Surely, one of the lessons of growing older is that it's highly desirable, when you are in your retirement years, to be close to family. Because illness is always a possibility, you never know when you might need help. It might be help with simple things, like getting to a doctor's appointment or going to the supermarket. Or, on a more serious note, it might be the help and comfort of having family members nearby when you go into the hospital for surgery.

Being close to family has many dimensions, of course. For many retirees, including me, the opportunity to spend time with children, and especially with grandchildren, can be the best part of retirement. I like to think it is rewarding for the grandchildren as well. Even so, a discussion of retirees who move—or who don't move—always comes down to this old idea: "Different strokes for different folks." The decision to move or to stay is very much an individual matter, and each retiree has to make his or her own judgment on where to go—or whether to go at all.

Our Florida investigation

A year after I retired, Sara and I thought seriously about leaving the Washington, D.C., area and moving to Florida. There were at least a couple of good reasons to make the move: We would get away from the ice and snow of Washington winters. And we would be closer to many of our relatives and friends who live in the Sunshine State, including Sara's four sisters.

But there were also several good reasons to stay: We had lived in the Washington area for more than 25 years. Our children and grandchildren were all nearby. So were the doctors and dentists we'd used for many years. We also felt very much at home. We had become attached to the city's great monuments and cultural attractions. And we liked the small communities of suburban Maryland and Virginia.

The idea of moving also raised several hard questions. First, were we ready to put forth the physical and psychological effort that moving requires? Only a few years earlier, we had sold our big five-bedroom house and moved to a small two-bedroom apartment in our retirement community. The memory of that move was fresh in our minds, and I, for one, wasn't sure I was ready for another move.

Second, what would it cost us to move to south Florida? Where would we live? How much would we have to spend for housing? And how would the cost of living in Florida compare with the cost of living in the Washington area?

These are the kinds of questions that face all retirees who are thinking of moving, whether they're considering the Sunbelt areas of the country, such as Florida and Arizona, or the newly popular retirement communities of the West and Pacific Northwest. One thing is sure: no matter where you want to go to retire, choosing a place to live requires a considerable amount of research. Frankly, the process is pretty much the same whether you are heading north, south, east, or west.

Sara and I did some in-depth research when we were thinking of moving to south Florida. The process would have been the same if we had been going to any other area of the country. You could easily repeat this type of research for any destination that interests you. In any event, this is what we did.

We took a trip to south Florida and spent three weeks in Broward County and Palm Beach County, where we made a fairly intensive effort to get to know the local communities. Although the weather in the region can be unpredictable at times, we were there during a period of warmth and sunshine.

Clearly, Florida's biggest drawing card is a pleasant climate during the winter months. In mid-February, I swam and played golf under blue skies and bright sunshine, with temperatures in the eighties. I wore short-sleeve shirts and shorts on days that my friends at home were dressed in parkas and using their snow shovels to dig out from under a big storm.

In the course of our visit, Sara and I tried to get a sense of what it would be like to live in Florida full-time. I was particularly interested in whether it would be cheaper to live in Florida than in the high-priced Washington area. Cost was important to us, as it probably will be to you, because, like many retirees, Sara and I are trying to make our retirement dollars last as long as possible.

Cheaper housing, smaller tax bills

To get a line on the cost of housing in south Florida, we visited several new housing developments. We studied and compared prices and the quality of the housing being offered. We also tried to find out as much as we could about the local communities and the facilities and services that were available to residents.

We talked with friends and relatives about their housing experiences in south Florida. At the time, it seemed clear to me that housing in south Florida was much less expensive than housing in the Washington, D.C., area. A few years later, when the national housing boom began, home prices in Florida rose rapidly, as they did everywhere else. Then, when the housing boom went bust, Florida homeowners suffered as home prices fell sharply and the state racked up a large number of foreclosures. At this point in mid-2009, an accurate comparison of housing costs in Florida versus costs in other states will have to wait until both the economy and the housing market recover.

During our trip to Florida, I asked my former Maryland neighbor, Walter Packer of Boynton Beach, about the cost of food in Florida compared to Maryland. Packer, who spent 25 years in the grocery business, had a keen eye for food prices and quality. Packer said at the time that he found fruits and vegetables in Florida were 20 percent cheaper and groceries generally 10 to 15 percent cheaper than in Maryland. Restaurant meals in Florida also tend to be less costly, Packer said, especially during "early bird" seating hours, which usually start around 5 p.m. or 5:30 p.m. These reduced-price meals are so popular that the "early bird" has been jokingly dubbed the state bird of Florida.

When I looked at the price of clothing in Florida, it seemed to be about the same as in Maryland. But we wouldn't need winter wardrobes, although we would need additional summer clothes. Then there was the matter of how much it would cost us to relocate. I was sure that it would cost several thousand dollars, but at that point I had not yet tried to come up with a firm figure.

When I got home from south Florida, I continued my research by phone and found that if we moved, we would save quite a bit of money on taxes. That was chiefly because Florida, unlike Maryland, Virginia, and the District of Columbia, has no state income taxes. That could mean a significant saving for us, since we are residents of Maryland. I knew how much I paid each year in Maryland taxes, but as a journalist, I was curious how much retired couples living in the D.C. area paid in state taxes.

I asked certified public accountant and tax expert William A. Fritz, Jr., of Fritz & Co. in Fairfax City, Virginia, to help me figure it out. We made these assumptions: the couples were over 65 and had annual incomes before taxes of $77,000, with $30,000 coming from Social Security, $42,000 from pensions, and $5,000 from interest on investments.

Based on 2008 state income tax rates, if the couples take the standard deductions, Bill Fritz said, they would pay state income taxes of $2,381 in Maryland, $1,980 in the District, and $547 in Virginia. By moving to Florida, the couples would save those amounts. The Virginia tax is considerably lower, Fritz told me, because the state grants a $12,000 "age deduction" for individuals over 65. Thus, a Virginia couple could get a $24,000 deduction. However, this age deduction phases out at certain income levels for individuals born after January 2, 1939. Single taxpayers lose $1 of the deduction for every $1 that their adjusted federal adjusted gross income (AFAGI) exceeds $50,000. For married couples, the dollar-for-dollar loss begins when their AFAGI exceeds $75,000.

In recent years, the tax picture in Florida has improved for anyone thinking of moving to the Sunshine State, according to Martin R. Glickstein, a certified public accountant in Maitland, Florida. First, the Florida intangible tax was repealed in 2006. Second, in 2008, Florida increased the state's homestead exemption from $25,000 to $50,000.

The intangible tax was a tax on an individual's total investments, including stocks, bonds, mutual funds, and money market funds. The state did not count bank deposits, certificates of deposit, annuities, U.S. government obligations, Florida state or municipal bonds, or retirement accounts such as 401(k) or Keogh plans. Intangible taxes remain in effect on certain commercial-style real estate investments.

Meanwhile, legal residents of Florida have seen an improvement in the homestead exemption on their personal residences. This feature reduces the assessed valuation of a house by up to

$50,000, which, in turn, reduces the homeowner's tax bill. The first $25,000 reduction applies to all property taxes, including school district taxes. The second $25,000 reduction applies to the assessed value between $50,000 and $75,000 and only to nonschool taxes.

As regards general sales taxes in the Washington region compared to Florida, this is how they stack up. Maryland has a 6 percent tax, Virginia's tax is 5 percent, and the District's tax is 5.75 percent. The Florida tax is 6 percent. However, some counties in Florida add sales surcharges of up to 1.5 percent.

Moving and adjusting

As Sara and I mulled over the idea of moving to Florida, we talked about the process of adjusting to a new state and a new community. We realized that if we moved, we'd have to adjust not only to a new climate but to a new home, new geography, new cities and towns, new highways, new newspapers and TV stations, new libraries, new businesses, and new customs. For instance, while I was visiting Florida, I couldn't find a bank that was open on Saturdays, and that was rather annoying.

Of course, before we moved, we would have to sell our apartment in Maryland and buy a new home or apartment in Florida and then furnish it. That would be a guaranteed hassle that would discourage me but probably not Sara. She is a very good organizer and handled our last move quite efficiently.

As I mentioned, we sold the house we lived in for 25 years and moved five miles away to our present condominium apartment in a high-rise building. But I can easily remember the feeling of loss when we left the old neighborhood, with its familiar faces and shopkeepers who called you by your first name. And I can also remember the strangeness of getting used to a new home in new surroundings, even though we hadn't moved a great distance.

One possible alternative to a full-fledged move was to become a "snowbird"—someone who goes south in the winter and north in the summer. That is what some of our friends and relatives did. They bought small and relatively inexpensive apartments in Florida, often fully furnished, which they use for three or four months during the winter. But they keep their homes in the Northeast and thus do not have to deal with Florida weather in the summer.

That would mean finding the money for a second home. If we could do so, the arrangement would have many advantages. We'd be close to our children and grandchildren in the North most of the year. Indeed, they'd probably insist on coming to Florida to visit us during winter holidays! We'd be close to our Florida relatives for several months—long enough to enjoy their company but not long enough to wear out our welcome.

Sara, however, was dubious about having two homes to worry about. Not only would it be a financial strain, she said, but she feared that problems could arise in either home when we were away at the other. So we slowly dropped the idea of having two homes.

That left one option: a full-time move to Florida. Several neighbors had recently done that, and they reported that things had worked out well for them. While we were weighing the pros and cons of making the big move, several other factors began to dominate our thinking and eventually persuaded us to stay in the Washington area. Those factors involved our children and, especially, our grandchildren.

When I discussed relocating in one of my *Washington Post* columns, I received a dozen letters from readers offering their opinions. One of the most persuasive letters came from a woman who told us about her mother's move to Florida.

Although her mother came north to visit occasionally, the daughter said, her mother missed seeing her grandchildren grow up and in many ways lost touch with her daughter's family.

The message in the letter was clear: don't do it. The more we talked about moving, the more we came back to the question of whether a move would cause us to lose touch with our young grandchildren. We kept thinking of that old saying, "Out of sight, out of mind."

But there was one other important factor: if the time came when one of us became seriously ill, we did not want to be living in Florida, far from our children. That would force our kids to fly to Florida to deal with our health problems.

Sara and I had been through that experience with my parents, who were occasional snowbirds. When my father became ill, Sara and I went to Florida to bring them back to our home. When Sara's brother became seriously ill, his son spent many weeks commuting between New York and Florida. We had seen many other examples of that kind of event.

Finally, when we weighed all our reasons for moving against all our reasons for staying, we decided to stay.

Choosing a place to live

When Sara and I thought about moving, we considered going to Florida because of its climate and cost-of-living advantages. It was also where many of our friends and relatives lived. We felt that if we were going to make a major move at a late stage of life, it is reassuring to be close to family and friends.

But wherever you may want to go to retire, you are likely to face the same kinds of questions and dilemmas that we faced. Also, choosing a retirement community is no easy task. Ask David Savageau. For nearly three decades, this Denver native has been studying and writing about the best retirement communities in America. He is the author of *Retirement Places Rated, 7th Edition* (Wiley, 2007), a 302-page book that profiles 200 retirement areas across the United States and rates them for ambience, living costs, climate, services, personal safety, work opportunities, and housing.

When I came across Savageau's book, I was awed by the extraordinary amount of research that went into its creation. As a reporter who has spent his life gathering information, I could appreciate the effort involved. So I was anxious to meet Savageau and get his thoughts about why retirees do or do not move and why some moves are successful and others are not.

Savageau has traveled extensively in the United States and has visited nearly every one of the 200 areas he has written about. In the course of his wanderings with his wife, Karyl, and a silver Airstream trailer in tow, he has had an opportunity to talk to many retirees about their relocation experiences, both good and bad. Savageau says people who are thinking about relocating should begin to plan their move long before they retire. "The decision to relocate should require at least five years in advance of the official day of retirement," he observes.

There is a well-established process that many people use to prepare for a retirement move, according to Savageau. Commonly, they spend vacations, both short and long, in an area they find attractive. In time, they may acquire a second home in the area, spending more and more time there in order to see whether they would be comfortable living there year round.

People need sufficient time, Savageau points out, to develop "a sense of place." Some people, he notes, make the mistake of simply moving to Florida or Arizona without doing any homework. When they find they don't like the hot summers or the traffic congestion or other aspects of those areas, they move again and again until they wind up back where they started, saying, "There's no place like home."

Despite all the talk about moving, Savageau says, U.S. Census Bureau figures usually show less than 5 percent of people over 60 moved between states over the past two decades. Since 2008, however, relocating for retirement has dropped because of the slowing economy and the difficulty of selling homes. There is a positive side to the slump, though. Home prices have fallen the sharpest in the traditional retirement states of California, Nevada, Arizona, and Florida, and some careful shopping can uncover sale or rental bargains.

When he first began studying mobility patterns nearly 30 years ago, Savageau says, climate was the main reason that retirees moved, and almost all the movement was to the Sunbelt states. While climate is still a factor today, he notes, cost of living is now the major reason for relocation. The desire to save money prompts many retirees to go to less expensive communities where housing is cheaper and taxes are lower. Another factor rising in importance: interesting part-time or seasonal opportunities for work.

Retirees also are expanding their range of destinations, with the Pacific Northwest, Rocky Mountains, and New England becoming popular relocation choices. Savageau has counted 42 states that are now seeing newcomers. Indeed, he says, before you move to any retirement community, find out whether you are likely to be welcomed by local residents. If the community is not hospitable to newcomers, you may not want to move there.

Places that are used to seeing and welcoming newcomers include college towns, areas near military bases, and vacation and resort areas. Lately, a small trend has started among suburbanites who prefer to downsize but don't want to leave a familiar area—so they retire downtown, perhaps to a former hotel or department store that's been converted to condominiums. It is in all of those places, Savageau suggests, that retirees are likely to find it relatively easy to make new friends. Making new friends and developing a satisfying social life are vital to any successful relocation, he says.

Trying to find friends fast

I know what Savageau is talking about. Although Sara and I did not move to Florida, we did move locally to a brand-new 300-family apartment complex in a retirement community. We found ourselves among a diverse group of people who had one main thing in common: they were all new residents. And they all wanted to make friends fast.

This was our third such experience. On two previous occasions, we moved to new single-family housing developments where, each time, everybody in the neighborhood was new, and they too all wanted to make friends fast. What happens in these circumstances is a lot like the Great Land Rush. Your phone begins to ring with calls from your new neighbors, and your mailbox is soon stuffed with invitations for cocktails, brunch, and dinner. Then the games begin. It may be poker, bridge, canasta, or mah-jongg. After that, you begin to get invitations to join a club: the Lions or the Kiwanis or Rotary or Knights of Columbus or American Legion, and so on.

Then you hear from the fun bunch. "We're going to the water-walking class on Wednesdays. Would you like to join us?" Or, "We need a few more singers in our little theater group. We're doing *The Mikado*. Won't you come down and try out?" That's how it all begins. You can probably guess how most of these overtures will end.

At the cocktail party, your new neighbors all seemed like they'd rather be someplace else, except for the guy in the corner. You spent most of the evening listening to him talk about his gall bladder surgery. His story took longer than the operation.

At the dinner party, the food was good. But the other three couples all seemed to know each other from their old neighborhood, so they spent most of the evening talking about people and places they all knew. None of it meant anything to you.

At the brunch, you met an interesting couple, and it seemed like you could be friends. The only problem was that they spent most of their time on cruises. In fact, they were heading out the next morning on their forty-third cruise. It didn't seem like they'd have much time to spend with you.

You joined the poker game and played for about six weeks, but you quit because one of the players complained constantly about his bad luck. So you made an excuse about working late and left. The canasta game also broke up about a month after it began, because two of the players said the other two players were too slow.

Friends were easier to find at the service clubs and at the fraternal organizations. And although you didn't get a singing role in *The Mikado*, it was fun helping with the costumes, and you became friendly with several people who, coincidentally, had joined the water-walking class. So you joined, too.

In any event, a couple of years after we moved to each of our new communities, we had a whole new set of friends. Of course, they didn't include any of the people we first met when we arrived. We found friends in our own way and at our own pace.

That outcome is very much in keeping with research findings gathered by Cathy Goodwin, an independent career and business consultant living in Seattle, Washington. Goodwin is the author of *Making the Big Move* (New Harbinger Publications, 1999). Although out of print, the book is available at some booksellers and at http://www.RelocationStrategy.com. Goodwin has lived all over North America, from Connecticut to California and from Alaska to Florida. Having moved frequently, she has developed a keen sense of what it takes to adjust to life in a new community.

Goodwin is a strong believer in the take-it-slow approach. All too often, she says, new arrivals rush to get involved in community activities and make new friends. "There's a real tendency to charge in and say, 'I want to feel at home right away.'" But that's not the way to go, she adds. "It takes two years at a minimum to feel at home in a new place."

Goodwin suggests that people wait a while before trying to make new friends or getting involved with volunteer activities. She reasons as follows: the people you initially become friendly with after you move in are unlikely to still be your friends by the time your second year rolls around. By then, you probably will have found friends you like better. But by then, it may be difficult to get away from some of your earlier acquaintances.

The same rule applies when it comes to volunteering for community activities, Goodwin says. It's a good idea to wait until you become familiar with the volunteer opportunities that are available. Some volunteer jobs will be far more interesting than others. "When you're new, you don't know what the good stuff is." And if you don't wait long enough to find out, she adds, you could lock yourself into activities that might be hard to get out of.

Of course, if you don't move, you won't have to worry about finding new friends. But many retirees do move, and for good reasons. And the evidence is that they find communities and friends they enjoy and are happy that they made the move. It can be done. Just look before you leap.

For more information

Goodwin, Cathy, *Making the Big Move*, Oakland, CA: New Harbinger Publications, Inc., 1999.

Howells, John, *Where to Retire: America's Best and Most Affordable Places*, 6th Edition, Guilford, CT: Globe Pequot Press, 2006.

Savageau, David, *Retirement Places Rated*, 7th Edition, Hoboken, NJ: John Wiley and Sons, 2007.

DECISION 11

How should I arrange my estate to save on taxes and avoid probate?

Living in a retirement village has many advantages: no grass to mow, no leaves to rake, and no snow to shovel. It also has some drawbacks, one of which is that we live among a large group of elderly people. Thus, it is not unusual to hear that one of our neighbors has died. While we are sad to hear such news, we are not surprised. The people who live in this community are in their sixties, seventies, and eighties. Some are even in their nineties. And while most of the people we know lead active, busy lives, we are aware that sooner or later the aging process will take its toll.

For Sara and me, the deaths of neighbors are reminders of our own physical vulnerabilities. Although we're both feeling well, the memory of our medical experiences has focused our attention on whether we are properly prepared for the day—hopefully, far off—when one or both of us will die.

In this complicated world, we have discovered that death is not only an emotional event, it is also a legal event and even a taxable one. A favorable outcome depends on advance planning, getting good advice, and carefully assembling your financial records and documents.

The decision to organize our financial and family affairs did not come easily. Like most people, we weren't eager to think about dying. And there was even less incentive to think about wills and trusts and estate taxes, subjects that ordinarily would make our eyes glaze over. But Sara and I talked it over and decided that whether we liked it or not, one of these days we would have to depart. That being the case, we wanted to do what we could to achieve three goals: One, we wanted to depart in a neat and orderly way, creating the least amount of stress for our children. Two, we wanted to make sure that our heirs would get what we wanted them to get. Three, we wanted our estate to be settled with the smallest possible tax bill and the least amount of hassle.

To do all that, we got some good advice and made a series of decisions that will, we believe, accomplish those goals. Our guide through this legal jungle was Rhonda J. Macdonald, an attorney and certified public accountant whose office is in Vienna, Virginia. Macdonald is a specialist in wills, trusts, and other estate-planning matters.

I think it is fair to say that the process we went through in making our estate-planning decisions was a learning experience. Sara and I both learned many things we never knew about what the law requires and about the opportunities that the law offers. And as a journalist writing about retirement-related matters, I learned things from other experts in estate planning that were both useful and surprising. In the course of this chapter, I will try to convey an understanding of what Sara and I did and what we learned.

It goes without saying that the experience of making an estate plan did not make me, in any sense, an expert on the subject. The story of what we did is merely that and no more. It is certainly not a complete guide to estate planning. In fact, many aspects of estate planning are not even mentioned here, because we did not deal with them. Thus, if and when you focus on this aspect of retirement, you might have a very different experience from the one we had.

Planning ahead

The first thing that Sara and I did, even before we talked with Macdonald, was to arrange our funerals. We have a family burial plot, so we know where we're going to be laid to rest. By making the arrangements with a funeral home in advance, we were able to negotiate the price and lock it in. This means that there'll be no additional charges, even if our funerals take place years from now. Also, we'll be able to pay for the cost over the next several years. All this means that our children won't have to rush around and make funeral arrangements in a crisis atmosphere. I've seen that happen to other people, and it's an unhappy sight.

But planning for your funeral is not—pardon the pun—the end of the story. Unfortunately, you also have to get ready for what happens before you die. Often, that involves a period of illness that may require its own kind of preparation.

When Sara and I met with Macdonald for the first time, we talked about what would happen if either of us became seriously ill to the point where we could no longer make our own decisions about our medical treatment. Macdonald recommended that we sign a document called an advance medical directive. In my case, it allows me to name Sara as the single individual who can make all my health-care decisions for me if I am physically or mentally unable to do so. It also allows me to name an alternate person if she is not available.

Medical directives, Macdonald said, vary by state. Some states have a medical power of attorney and others a living will. In Virginia, where Macdonald is based, both types of medical directives have been combined into a single document called an "advance medical directive." The main purpose of my own advance medical directive is to make it clear that I do not want my doctors to keep me on life-support equipment or procedures if they decide that I have a terminal condition or that I am in a "persistent coma" from which there is no reasonable possibility of recovery. In those cases, I want them to understand that I would prefer to die naturally. Since I would be unable to tell that to my doctors directly, I also make it clear that I am relying on the document itself to be "the final expression of my legal right to refuse medical or surgical treatment."

While the wording of my document fully expresses my wishes and my hope that the doctors will follow my wishes, it isn't quite that simple. Macdonald explained that in virtually every hospital there is an ethics or other committee that will make the final decision on whether to "pull the plug" on a patient for whom there is no hope of recovery. That may take some time if the patient shows even the smallest life sign.

In my advance medical directive, it says that before any life-ending action can be taken, a medical team must decide whether I am able to make my own health-care decisions. This determination is to be made by my physician, along with a second physician or clinical psychologist. After they examine me, they must submit a report in writing. Until they do, they can't withhold or withdraw treatment.

What role does my wife play in all this? As mentioned, in my directive I have given her the power to make all my health-care decisions for me if I am unable to do so. These can be trivial decisions about my reactions to medication or far-reaching decisions about terminating my life. She is, in fact, authorized to make almost any medical decision for me, and she even has the power to direct the writing of a "no code" or "do not resuscitate" order. (Incidentally, when Sara signed her advance medical directive, she named me as her representative and gave me similar powers.)

Because Macdonald has her office in Virginia, the advance medical directive that we signed is a Virginia version. Macdonald noted that these directives vary from state to state, but added, "My experience, happily, has been that a living will validly executed in any state is honored in another state."

A matter of trust

On more than one occasion over the years, Sara and I have watched friends and relatives try to deal with one of life's most difficult problems: the mental incapacitation of a spouse or parent because of a stroke or the swift onset of Alzheimer's disease. When that happens, especially because of a stroke, the stricken individual may suddenly lose his or her ability to make informed legal and financial decisions. What is needed, therefore, is a way to appoint a spouse or child to make those decisions for the person who is ill. That way, Macdonald told us, is to sign a general durable power of attorney, a document that allows Sara and me to appoint each other to act for each other in the event that either one of us can no longer make our own financial and legal decisions. In a way, the durable power of attorney resembles our advance medical directives—except that the durable power of attorney deals with financial matters rather than health matters.

The powers granted in a durable power of attorney are extremely broad. In essence, Sara and I have given each other almost complete power over the financial side of our lives. For instance, my power of attorney allows my wife to gain access to my bank accounts, to manage or even sell my real estate, to sell or transfer my investments, and more. And, of course, Sara has given me the same powers.

While these powers are sweeping, Macdonald said, they often are needed in a hurry when a spouse becomes mentally incapacitated. Even so, she said, the original document should be kept in a safe place from which it will not be removed until the person who signed it becomes incapacitated. Macdonald cautioned us that such documents become effective immediately when you sign them, not just when you become ill. She said she tells clients that they should have a high level of trust in the person to whom they give their power of attorney. In other words, make sure you really trust each other.

Those sweetheart wills

At this point, Sara and I were feeling somewhat self-satisfied with our progress. We'd been able to make advance funeral plans, and we managed to understand and sign two complicated legal documents: medical directives and powers of attorney. But as we soon discovered, that was only the beginning of our learning experience in estate planning. We had a long way to go.

Essentially, we were taking a quick course in wills, trusts, and estate taxes. Macdonald was a patient instructor, always willing to explain an obscure concept over and over again until we understood. And there was much to understand. Estate planning is an extremely complicated field, especially for a person who is not a lawyer and can't even do his own tax return. But thanks to Macdonald, I finally began to understand that estate planning has many advantages.

Macdonald says that married people who come to see her often bring her what she calls "sweetheart wills." That's the kind of will in which the husband leaves everything to his wife and the wife leaves everything to her husband. Indeed, that's the kind of will that Sara and I each had before we began to work with Macdonald.

Here's how sweetheart wills work: if I die, I can leave everything I own to Sara, tax free, at least from a federal tax viewpoint. The problem arises when she dies. At that point, the total dollar value of her estate, less any available federal and state estate tax exemptions, may be subject to estate taxes. Thus, while a sweetheart will is romantic, it may not keep Uncle Sam or your home state from taking a bite out of your estate after a second spouse dies. Nor will it avoid the expense and delays of going through probate court.

What is probate? Generally speaking, it's a legal process that is used to wind up a deceased person's financial affairs. The personal representative or executor who is named in the will prepares an inventory of the assets and liabilities of the estate, pays any taxes and bills that are due, and makes sure that the heirs get the bequests that have been left to them. But all of those items have to be approved or at least reviewed by the court. Many people try to avoid probate court, if they can, because of the time it takes to settle an estate and the filing fees involved.

Macdonald told us that the best way to avoid or minimize both estate taxes and probate was to create a "revocable living trust" for each spouse, which is used to hold the assets belonging to each. The trust also constitutes what is called a "bypass trust," meaning that when each partner dies, the assets in the trust will escape federal taxes up to a certain dollar limit—although state taxes may be due.

Now, even after we decided to create two living trusts, Sara and I still needed wills. In our wills, we each named a personal representative and specified their duties. Our wills describe how we want our personal property to be distributed and give other instructions on winding up our financial affairs. However, detailed instructions about who inherits what and when and how are all stated in our trust documents.

By creating two bypass trusts, we were setting the stage so we could take advantage of a currently available federal tax exemption. This exemption provides that, during life and/or after death, each spouse can transfer a certain amount of money to children or other beneficiaries without incurring gift or estate taxes.

The estate tax: a strange story

Congress adopted the Tax Act of 2001 following a campaign by business interests to reduce and eventually repeal the estate tax. The Tax Act slowly increased the annual tax exemption until it reached $3.5 million for deaths occurring in 2009. It then repealed the estate tax for deaths occurring in 2010. In an odd legislative twist, however, the law also said that unless Congress amended or reenacted the Tax Act of 2001, the estate tax would spring back to life with a $1 million exemption for deaths occurring in 2011 or later.

In late 2009, with the clock ticking, Congress had not yet made a decision on how to avoid letting 2010 become a year without any estate tax. Indeed, there were endless jokes about 2010 being the best year to die because no taxes would be due.

President Obama proposed a permanent $3.5 million tax exemption and a 45 percent top tax rate, and there were signs that Congress might go along—or might agree to a one-year extension of the $3.5 million exemption. But the outcome was uncertain as this book went to press in late 2009.

However, this is the way the bypass trust system works at this time: If a husband dies first, the bypass trust shelters his estate tax exemption from estate taxes and from probate. When his wife dies, the trust shelters her estate tax exemption from estate taxes and probate. That allows an amount equal to double the estate tax exemption to be distributed to the couple's beneficiaries without federal estate taxes. Depending on where the couple lived, however, state taxes may be a factor.

By comparison, Macdonald says, having only sweetheart wills is very expensive for a couple with assets (including life insurance) exceeding the estate tax exemption. When the husband dies, everything goes to his wife tax free. The tax problem arises when the wife dies and can claim only one exemption. Assuming a $3.5 million federal estate tax exemption and assets totaling $7 million when the second spouse dies, the estate would have to pay almost $1.6 million in estate taxes if only sweetheart wills are in place, compared to zero estate tax if bypass trusts are in place.

Importantly, with a $3.5 million exemption, there is a flat 45 percent tax rate on anything owed at death over and above the amount of the exemption. If both spouses put their assets in trust, they get two exemptions instead of one and pay no taxes.

To avoid probate, a couple must transfer their assets into their trusts. The transfers of money or property involve a process called "re-titling." The idea is to divide the couple's assets as equally as possible into the two trusts. For instance, a joint brokerage account that reads "John and Mary Jones" would be divided and changed to, "John Jones, Revocable Trust" and "Mary Jones, Revocable Trust"—thus shifting those assets into two trusts. The deed for a house that is owned jointly also would be revised, Macdonald says. The house could be put into the trust of the spouse with the lesser amount of total assets, but both spouses would retain the same rights to use the house, or even sell it, as before.

When Sara and I did our trusts, we put one-half of our condominium apartment in her trust, one-half in my trust. We re-titled our brokerage account but not our IRA accounts. If I were to die first, Sara would be allowed to roll over my IRAs into her IRAs, so no re-titling was necessary. I could do the same if she were to die first.

While trusts make a lot of sense, they have a few drawbacks. Typically, it costs $3,000 to $5,000 to have an estate-planning lawyer set up trusts for a married couple and do some of the legal work that goes with it. And the job of re-titling assets can be complicated and time-consuming. Worse, it may make some people feel that they've lost control of their assets, even though they haven't. In our case, the re-titling procedure was a bit tedious, but it was completed in a couple of months.

One of the main arguments for creating a trust is to avoid the time and expense of probate. But many states now have adopted a fast-track system for probate, especially for small estates, and that has made the process easier.

Would it be worthwhile for you to create a bypass trust? That depends on the size of your estate and what changes, if any, Congress makes in the estate tax law. Check with an estate planner to make sure.

Getting yourself organized

How do you know what your estate is worth? Here's my two-step plan for measuring the value of your estate and organizing your financial information.

STEP ONE

Take a personal financial inventory by adding up everything you own and everything you owe. If you're married, make three lists. First, list the assets and liabilities that are in your name only; second, list those in your spouse's name only; and third, list those assets that you own jointly. When you're done, subtract what is owed from what is owned on all three lists. That will give you a rough idea of the value of your estate, your spouse's estate, and your shared estate.

Typically, a list of assets will include bank accounts, certificates of deposit, stocks, bonds, and mutual funds. The value of your life insurance also should be listed. Include the fair market value of your home, car, boat, home furnishings, jewelry, real estate, and pension accounts. A list of liabilities would include any money you owe, including your mortgage, bank loans, car loans, and credit card balances.

STEP TWO

Think for a moment of how hard it would be for your spouse or your children to find all your personal and financial information if you weren't around. You can spare them a lot of grief by doing the job for them. I suggest keeping your information and documents where they are safe and easy to find. A fireproof file cabinet or home safe may be better than a safe-deposit box.

Start by locating your will and trust documents. If you have prearranged your funeral, include the name and phone number of the funeral home, the agreements you signed, and a record of your payments. Among the documents that should be in your file are the deed to your home or other property you own, the title to your car, your military discharge and veterans' benefit papers, marriage license, divorce papers, birth certificates, citizenship papers, passports, and immigration papers. Also, you should include your bank, brokerage, and mutual fund account numbers and the addresses or phone numbers of those institutions, as well as your credit card numbers, balances, and phone numbers. Finally, include your Social Security number, the amount of your monthly payments and, if you have direct deposit, the name of the bank to which the check is sent. Do the same for pension payments.

Make sure that a family member knows where you keep the key to your safe-deposit box and the name of the bank where the box is located. Make a list of what's in your box. Also, list the names, numbers, and details of all your insurance policies, especially life, auto, and homeowners policies. And don't forget health insurance and nursing home policies. Make a list of your doctors and their phone numbers, too. By the way, once you've done all these things, make sure to tell your spouse, children, or other relatives what you've done and where they can find all the information.

As Sara is fond of saying, "Preparedness is next to godliness."

Thinking about the unthinkable

Unfortunately, when it comes to deciding what will happen to your money and your property after you die, you can do everything right and still come out wrong.

Any lawyer who has practiced estate law for any length of time can tell stories of parents who tried to do the right thing by leaving their money and property to their children in equal shares, believing that the show of fairness would help maintain family harmony after they died. But all too often, it doesn't work out that way.

"When it comes to money, family loyalty goes out the window," I was told by Jeffrey L. Condon, a Santa Monica, California, estate lawyer, who talked about the conflicts that can arise after parents die. The children are not just the parents' children anymore, Condon said, "They're people dividing money." And that often makes them behave differently from the way they would if their parents were still alive.

Condon told the story of a couple who left everything they owned equally to their three children. However, years earlier, they had spent $250,000 to send one son to medical school. Another son attended a local junior college, while the daughter did not go to college.

After the parents' death, the discrepancy in education spending caused a rift among the siblings. The brother and sister of the doctor felt that he should give them part of his inheritance to equalize what their parents spent on all three. The doctor disagreed; he no longer speaks to his siblings.

What the parents should have done, Condon said, was to equalize their spending on their children during their lifetime. Parents who occasionally help a child financially tend to forget about unequal treatment, Condon said. "But rest assured, your children haven't forgotten. And they're keeping score." Condon and his father, attorney Gerald M. Condon, told the story in their book *Beyond the Grave: The Right Way and the Wrong Way of Leaving Money to Your Children (and Others)*, Revised Edition (Harper Business, 2001).

Family strife can arise out of many inheritance scenarios. Second marriages, especially those involving widows and widowers with grown children, can be disasters waiting to happen. All too often, inheritances wind up in the wrong hands because of poor planning, failure to use the right legal tools, or just plain greed. Lawyers who specialize in wills, trusts, and estate planning say there are many ways to create inheritance problems. But there are also ways to prevent them. Here are a few examples:

Unequal shares

Parents often tell Rhonda Macdonald that they want to leave more money to one child than to another. Usually, the reason given is that one child is very successful and "doesn't need the money," while the other child is relatively poor. When Macdonald hears that, she tries to convince the parents that it's a bad idea to give unequal shares to their offspring simply for economic reasons. "By leaving a smaller share to your successful child, you are punishing him or her for success. And by leaving a greater share to your poorer child, you're rewarding his or her lack of success," Macdonald tells her clients. That argument seems to work, Macdonald said, and few of her clients wind up leaving their children unequal shares for economic reasons.

Second marriages

The classic horror story begins when Dad dies and Mom remarries. Mom and her second husband each have three grown children. They really want to leave their individual wealth to their own children, but they already have put all their savings and property in both names and thus own everything jointly. That means that if the second husband dies before Mom does, all their joint assets will automatically become Mom's property. It will then be up to Mom, in her will, to decide what his children and her children will get. And even if Mom leaves most of her second husband's assets to his children, they will have to wait until she dies to get their inheritance. That could take a long time, and his kids are likely to make a considerable fuss over the delay.

The easiest way to avoid these conflicts, Macdonald said, is for remarried spouses to keep their assets in their own names. That allows them to leave their individual money and property to their own children through their wills. If they've already put their assets in both names, they can go back and re-title them.

If Mom will need income to live on after her second husband dies, he can set up a trust for her that contains his assets, Macdonald said. Such a trust is called a "qualified terminable interest property," or QTIP trust. It allows Mom to receive income from her second husband's assets after his death. It can also guarantee that the principal of the trust ultimately will be inherited by the second husband's children, although, once again, they may have to wait until Mom dies.

In some cases, this may not be the complete story. For instance, in Virginia, Maryland, and the District of Columbia, Mom can claim one-third of her second husband's assets if he omits her from his will or leaves her less than one-third, even if the assets are held in his own name. This privilege can be waived with a premarital agreement.

Watch out for those in-laws

A couple in their eighties, Arthur and Mary, plan to leave their estate to their only son, Roger, who is 55. They hope their son, when he dies, will pass along his inheritance to their grandchildren. But they worry about what will happen if their son dies before his wife, Selma, who would then get her husband's inheritance. They are not sure if Selma actually would pass the inheritance along to the grandchildren. In fact, if Selma remarries, the inheritance could be passed along to her second husband and members of his family, and that's not what the grandparents have in mind.

One way for Arthur and Mary to protect their grandchildren's inheritance, according to Macdonald, is to create a generation-skipping trust, which will ensure that the couple's money goes to their grandchildren at a specified age. Here's how that would work: Their son, Roger, would become the trustee of the trust after the deaths of his mother and father. Roger would get the annual income generated by the trust or a percentage of the value of the trust each year. Roger could use as much of the principal of the trust as necessary to pay expenses for the health, education, and support of himself and his children.

A generation-skipping trust can have tax advantages. There is a generation-skipping tax exemption equal to the estate tax exemption, which can avoid estate taxation at Roger's death while guaranteeing an inheritance for his children.

That amount would be counted as part of Arthur or Mary's estate when the second spouse dies. Taxes would be paid on the total value of the estate, less the individual estate tax exemption.

When children owe money to their parents

Anger and confusion are almost inevitable when children borrow money from parents and don't pay it back. After the parents die, it is often unclear how much was borrowed, when and how the loans were to be repaid, and whether interest was to be charged. Worse yet, with the passage of time, children often start to think of the money they borrowed not as loans but gifts. On top of the confusion, Macdonald said, some of the children are likely to demand that their siblings repay their loans so that the total inheritance is not reduced by the debts.

Macdonald said she tries to head off these problems by asking clients, when they come in to write their wills, to give her the specific details of any loans they made to their children so she can include the information in the wills. That way, she said, when the parents die, the terms of the loans will be on record.

Naming the executors and trustees

When parents write their wills and create trusts, they often name children as personal representatives, executors, or trustees, making them responsible for placing a value on the assets of the estate, distributing the assets to the heirs, and filing various documents, including the deceased's final income tax. But how many children in a family should be given this task? The answer, says Macdonald, is "all of them." In Macdonald's experience, the offspring will not be happy if they are left out, no matter where in the world they are. They will want to be part of any decision affecting their inheritance, be it by phone, fax, or e-mail.

This is particularly true, Macdonald said, because executors and trustees are allowed to charge a fee for the work involved in settling their parents' estate. When there is more than one executor or trustee, the fee is shared. If only some of the children are named as executors and if they opt to receive executors' fees, Macdonald said, that may skew what otherwise would have been an equal division of assets among the children.

Getting the business

At times, parents flatly refuse to give equal shares of their estate to all their children. Often, that occurs when there is a family business. On those occasions, Macdonald said, parents may insist on leaving the firm to the offspring who have been working with them in the business for years. That may make the other children in a family unhappy, even though they chose to work in other fields. Indeed, those children might even sue on the grounds that they are getting a smaller inheritance than their siblings. If the parents think that such a lawsuit is likely, Macdonald said, they can attempt to head it off by inserting a "no contest" clause in their wills. Under that clause, if the children sue, they lose the inheritance they were slated to get. "If they sue, they get nothing," Macdonald said.

Disinheriting children

There are lots of reasons parents want to omit children from their wills or inheritance plans. The most common one is that a child is estranged and the parents haven't seen him or her for years; in some instances, the child has been involved with alcohol or drugs or has been in trouble with the law.

Jeffrey and Gerald Condon caution parents that if they omit a child from their will, one of two things is likely to happen: the child will either sue or become a burden to his or her siblings.

Although such lawsuits generally fail, they can be costly to the other children. In fact, the Condons noted, the other children may find it cheaper to settle than pay the legal costs involved.

Instead of cutting a child out of their will, the Condons advise, parents should put the child's share of the estate in a trust. The parents can then specify when and how their estranged son or daughter will get any money or income from the trust. The Condons also recommend that if parents omit a child from their wills, they should write a letter telling the child what they're doing. The letter may encourage the child to renew his or her ties with the family. At least, they say, it will give the child fair warning of what is going to happen.

Talking it out

Most lawyers agree that whatever inheritance or estate plan you adopt, it is important to explain your actions by discussing them with your children and with other relatives. Children should know exactly what their parents intend to do with their money and other assets. If they have problems with the parents' plans, it's a good idea to find that out before it's too late.

For more information

Here are just a few sources of guidance on wills, trusts, and taxes.

Books

American Bar Association. *The American Bar Association Guide to Wills and Estates*, Third Edition, New York: Random House, 2009.

Condon, Jeffrey L., and Gerald M. Condon, *Beyond the Grave: The Right Way and the Wrong Way of Leaving Money to Your Children (and Others)*, Revised Edition, New York: Harper Business, 2001.

Palermo, Michael T., *AARP Crash Course in Estate Planning* (Updated), New York: Sterling, 2008.

Ventura, John, *Kiplinger's Estate Planning*, New York: Kaplan Publishing, 2008.

Web Sites

National Association of Financial and Estate Planning: www.nafep.com. Click on "Estate Planning Basics."

Nolo Press: www.nolo.com. Click on "Wills, Trusts and Estate Planning."

How can I age successfully?

At some point in our lives, we all have to admit to ourselves that we are growing older. Signs of aging creep up on us in subtle ways. Gray hairs show up in our thirties. We need bifocals in our forties, a hearing aid in our fifties, and a heart bypass operation in our sixties. Then we start to have memory lapses. While they are merely annoying in our younger years, these lapses become scarier as we age.

In a way, even retirement is a sign of aging—not a physical one, perhaps, but an event that is usually related to increasing age. Whether we choose to retire at 62, at 66, or at 70, retirement usually occurs when we have completed about three-quarters of our life span. Thus, when we retire, it is clear that we're moving into the final quarter of our lives.

That is not meant to sound grim. In any football game, the last quarter is often the most exciting. So, too, with retirement. It is one more chance to add points on the scoreboard of your life. It is, in fact, a very special time of life, as many retirees have discovered. Indeed, in a survey for the National Council on the Aging, 49 percent of Americans age 65 to 69 said, "These are the best years of my life."

I can relate to that sentiment. The opportunity to write the "Retirement Journal" column after I retired—and its popularity—was the frosting on the cake of my career. Even the chance to put my ideas and experiences together in this book was a long-cherished ambition, realized at age 73. Yes, the clock is ticking. But it can tick for many years. As retirees, our primary challenge is to stay healthy long enough to enjoy the pleasures and opportunities that retirement can bring us.

Thanks to modern medicine and rising living standards, increases in life expectancy have been dramatic. As noted earlier, a 65-year-old woman can expect to live to 84, while a 65-year-old man can look forward to living until 81. Medical advances are steadily extending those frontiers. Living to 100 will soon be commonplace. But what does it take to reach those extended ages? As gerontologists and social scientists learn more about the aging process, they are able to provide us with increasingly better answers to that question.

I found some interesting ideas in a book about growing older, *Successful Aging*, by John W. Rowe and Robert L. Kahn. The book is based on the MacArthur Foundation Study of Aging in America, which took 10 years and cost $15 million. Among other things, the study looked closely at the history and habits of people who were aging well.

The book contains lots of good news for people in their sixties and seventies. The MacArthur study explodes many of the myths about aging and shows that, with proper diet, exercise, and medical care, elderly people can remain physically active and mentally alert for many years. Successful aging, the authors say, is based on three characteristics:

- A low risk of disease and disease-related disability
- High mental and physical abilities
- The desire to remain actively engaged with people

While heredity plays a role in longevity, the authors report that individual lifestyle choices and behavior over many years have the most influence on whether one ages well. Better yet, the authors tell us, it is never too late to change one's lifestyle for the better.

The lesson here is quite clear: the best way to prepare for a healthy old age is to follow a healthy lifestyle while you're young. But even if you didn't do that—I didn't start thinking about my health until I was in my fifties—there's still time.

Confronting illness

While there are many things we can do to preserve our health during retirement, we can't always avoid illness, which often strikes unexpectedly. I know this both from my own experience and from watching the ebb and flow of life in my retirement community, in which the average age is about 70 or 75. Hardly a month goes by that we don't hear about a friend or neighbor who has suffered a heart attack or a stroke or who has developed cancer.

In fact, I had my own medical battle, as I mentioned briefly in Chapter 8. Shortly after I retired, I decided that it was time to get a long-postponed physical checkup. The checkup led to the discovery of several clogged blood vessels in my heart. Although they had been partially cleared by angioplasty 10 years earlier, the blood vessels were now clogged again. My doctors said a four-way heart bypass operation was necessary.

I agreed to have the surgery, but the whole idea of having to undergo a serious operation so soon after I retired seemed truly unfair. I had worked for almost 45 years, and when I finally felt I was ready to retire, my health and perhaps even my life seemed to be in jeopardy.

The experience of going through open-heart surgery—and its aftermath—forced me to confront my own mortality in a way I had never done before. I wondered how long my retirement might last. And I asked myself, even if I survive, what will be the quality of my life?

Fortunately, I recovered from my surgery within a few months, but the experience left me feeling that if there was anything I wanted to do in retirement, I should do it quickly. This sense that my life might be limited was intensified by my wife's medical experience. Three years before my surgery, Sara underwent breast cancer surgery. She recovered after a nine-month ordeal involving chemotherapy. After her recovery, she decided to retire from her job at GE, where she had spent 22 years.

Thus, Sara and I both entered our retirement years after confronting major medical challenges. Sooner than most retirees, we had learned the truth of the old saying, "With good health, everything is possible. Without it, nothing is possible."

Pumping iron

After my heart surgery, my doctor sent me to a nearby cardiac rehabilitation center to improve my physical condition. It was there that I learned both aerobics and weight lifting. The first few weeks were rough, because my muscles were weak and my stamina was limited. But I slowly gained back my strength, and my physical condition improved. A dozen years later, I still invest time and energy in exercise. I tell my friends, especially those who trade stocks, that exercise is one of the few investments I've ever made that seems to have all upside and no downside.

In fact, until I went to the cardiac center, I didn't understand how easy it is to get hooked on regular exercise. My discovery came about this way: the center was open three days a week—Mondays, Wednesdays, and Fridays. So I would go to the center on those days and work out for about two hours a day. But after about four weeks at the center, I noticed something strange. On Tuesdays and Thursdays, I would wake up feeling restless. I wanted to exercise, but the center was closed. So I began making up my own exercises.

I soon figured out what was happening: exercise had become habit forming. And when I didn't exercise, my body missed it. Later, I read that natural chemicals called endorphins are released in the body during vigorous exercise. Endorphins can make us feel good and can even produce a feeling of euphoria, sometimes called "runner's high."

I don't know whether other people can get hooked on exercise as easily as I did, but the daily desire to work out made it much easier to get out of bed in the morning and go to the exercise room. I never had to fight the feeling of "Aw, skip it and go back to bed."

After I "graduated" from the cardiac center, I began to work out in the exercise room in our retirement community. The fitness center is located next door to our apartment building. In fact, it is so close that I'd have a hard time thinking of an excuse not to go regularly. Many of my fellow residents also use the exercise room, which was expanded recently because it is so popular. Until I retired, I had no idea that so many retirees devoted part of each day to exercise.

My routine is fairly simple: I walk a mile on the treadmill, in about 20 minutes. Then I spend 10 minutes on the rowing machine, 10 minutes on the stair climber, and about 20 minutes lifting dumbbells and working on the weight machines. As I work out, I see that many of my companions are walking faster, climbing higher, and lifting heavier weights than I do. But I feel no sense of competition. Many of these men and women are in their seventies and eighties, and I can only marvel at their determination to maintain their physical fitness.

Often, people who use the exercise room are recuperating from strokes, heart surgery, knee and hip replacements, and other assorted ailments. Others swim laps in the indoor swimming pool. Some do both.

For many residents, walking is the main form of exercise. On any decent day, the sidewalks and paths of my retirement community are crowded with walkers. A popular pastime is "walking the circle," the circle being a 3.2-mile path that goes around the community.

Some of my retired friends are "mall walkers." Each morning, they drive to a nearby indoor mall, walk rapidly around the shopping area for about an hour, and then gather for coffee and gossip. In inclement weather, I often hear the footsteps of the "hall walkers," residents of our building who get their exercise by walking up and down the corridors and steps of our 10-story building. I've done it; it takes about 45 minutes, and it makes for vigorous exercise.

Having discovered exercise late in life, I have no illusions about how I look when I'm lifting those dumbbells. When I glance in the wall mirror and see this gray-haired, aging man pumping iron, it's hard to keep from smiling. The sight reminds me of that old magazine ad for bodybuilder Charles Atlas, who boasted that he went from a "97-pound weakling" to "The World's Most Perfectly Developed Man." The ad featured a cartoon of a skinny kid on a beach who loses his girl to a sand-kicking muscle man and resolves to take weight-lifting lessons. As I struggle to lift those weights aloft, I sometimes hear myself saying, as did that kid, "Nobody's going to kick sand in my face!"

Do I wish I had started down the athletic trail 50 years ago? Yes, I do. But it wasn't as though I was a couch potato all my life. As a political reporter and columnist early in my career, I spent years running for campaign planes, trains, and buses. As a homeowner, I spent years mowing lawns, raking leaves, shoveling snow, and painting the house. Sure, it was all work, but it wasn't the kind of regular daily exercise that keeps your muscles toned and your heart healthy. If I had it to do over, I would make more time for exercise, especially because I've learned that exercise not only is good for your muscles but also is good for your brain. And what is good for your brain is good for your memory. And that's worth remembering.

My memory and me

The one thing that frightens me most about growing older is the idea that I might lose my memory. In fact, of all the questions I hear people ask about aging, the most frequent one is, "What's happening to my memory?" If you have ever watched a friend or loved one slip into Alzheimer's or dementia, as I have, you know the horror of the erosion of the human mind. I guess if I had a choice, I would prefer almost any other medical problem to losing my mental abilities. I'm sure many people feel the same way.

Memory is such an integral part of our personalities and individuality that it is unsettling to see signs that our memories are failing. In fact, not long ago, I began worrying about my memory after several incidents:

- I was shopping at the local mall when I ran into a man I'd worked with for many years, but I simply couldn't remember his name. It was on the tip of my tongue, but I couldn't dredge it out of my memory. I was embarrassed not to be able to call him by name.

- Another day, I drove to the supermarket, but when I came out, I couldn't remember where I had parked my car. I finally found it after wandering around for several minutes, but I was annoyed with myself.

- While at home, I walked from the kitchen into the bedroom to take care of a small chore. But when I got to the bedroom, I couldn't remember why I had gone in there. So I went back into the kitchen and remembered what I wanted to do in the bedroom.

- I took a phone message for my wife from her sister but didn't write it down because I was sure I would remember it. When Sara came home and asked if anybody had called, I said no. I had completely forgotten about her sister's call. Hours later, I remembered the call.

- Working at my desk, I found myself trying to recall the name of the capital of California. Once again, it was on the tip of my tongue, but it took a full five minutes before "Sacramento" swam into my consciousness.

After that "memorable" week, I started worrying about my memory. "What's going on here?" I asked myself. "Am I losing my memory? Does this have anything to do with my age?" I took my questions to Marilyn S. Albert, an expert in the field of aging and memory. She was quite reassuring.

"I wouldn't worry," Albert said after I told her about some of my recent memory lapses. Albert suggested a way to tell whether my occasional episodes of forgetfulness were serious or not. She put it this way:

"When you're reminded of the name you forgot or the location of your car and you can say, 'Yes, of course. That's it,' then you are probably fine," she said. "The real time to worry is when you find the name you forgot and you don't get the feeling that you knew it all along." I was happy to hear that, especially because I think I'm still in the "I knew it all along" camp. That little test also will be good news to my friends and acquaintances. Many people who live in my retirement community, I've noticed, are equally forgetful.

In fact, memory lapses are so common among my peers that they've been given a name. They are called "senior moments." If you listen to the conversations in the lobby, the exercise room, or the local clubhouse, you will hear a resident, in the midst of telling a story, pause and try to remember a name, place, or date. When that name, place, or date can't be recalled, the storyteller is likely to remark, "Oh, oh, I'm having a senior moment." It's usually said with some embarrassment, but no one is critical. The listeners simply nod sympathetically. It has happened to them, too.

Remembering people's names, Albert told me, represents a common difficulty. "We all forget them," she said. Memory, she noted, is embedded within many connections in the brain. The more such pathways, the easier it is to remember a name; the fewer the pathways, the harder it is to retrieve that name.

Names are often hard to remember because it is difficult to make an association with a "John" or a "Mary" when they are only names by themselves. To improve one's memory of a John or a Mary, an individual needs additional images or associations that will help create more pathways in the brain.

Albert said research has shown that there is a link between aging and memory. "We think [the two are] directly related," she said. Memory loss, she added, can be caused by changes in various areas of the brain that result in the loss of nerve cells and the shrinkage of brain tissue. However, Albert added, "The good news is that we have found that the nerve cells in the cortex are retained." The cortex plays a significant role in memory.

"What seems to be pretty clear is that as people get older, they have more trouble learning new information than younger people," Albert said. In addition, older people may be less inclined to think about cues that might help them remember, say, where they parked their cars—something younger people do spontaneously.

But older people can overcome these difficulties by working at remembering—for example, by deliberately fixing the location of their cars in their minds before they leave parking lots. Working at the business of remembering, Albert says, is a valuable strategy for older people. The evidence, Albert notes, is that once older people learn something—and learn it well—"they won't forget it any more rapidly than someone who is younger."

This ability to concentrate, retain information, and recall it, Albert said, is a key measure of the difference between benign and serious memory lapses. "When people are in the early stages of Alzheimer's," she said, "even if they make an extra effort to learn something, they will forget it." Albert estimates that 10 percent of the people in this country who are over age 65 have Alzheimer's. However, the total number of Alzheimer's cases is rising rapidly because the number of Americans over 65 is climbing steadily. The good news is that the scientific and medical communities are working tirelessly to find ways to alleviate and eventually cure Alzheimer's.

How to help your memory

In dealing with my moments of forgetfulness, I've found a number of memory aids and behavioral devices that can reduce the frustration of memory lapses. Here are some of the strategies that I use to get through the day:

- *The calendar.* I use a month-at-a-glance calendar with big boxes, so there is plenty of room to write down doctors' appointments, social engagements, upcoming birthdays, and so on. Before you make an appointment, make sure to check your calendar to avoid double booking. Then develop the habit of checking your calendar each evening, so you will know what you have to do tomorrow, where you are going, and what time you are expected.

- *A place for everything.* If you have trouble finding your car or house keys, your watch or sunglasses, do what Sara does. She has a special place for any item she is likely to need, and she makes sure that the item goes back to that special spot. That way, she knows exactly where to find her things and rarely has to search for anything. I'm less successful with that system than she is, but I'm trying.

- *Parking your car.* Many shopping center parking lots have numbered lanes or rows. When you park, make note of your location, and don't hesitate to jot it down. If there is no numbering system, look around and see where you are in relation to the nearest store, and fix that spot in your mind. That way, you'll be able to find your car easily.

- *Things to do.* The single biggest memory aid for both young and old is a list. To remember the things you want to do, make a list. A word of caution, however: one list is useful, but 10 lists only create confusion. When you develop your list, put the items in order of priority. And confine your list to the things you want to accomplish in the next week or 10 days. Once you've crossed off most of your immediate chores, you can start a new list and repeat the process.

- *Remembering names.* This is a tricky business because we know many people and know them under many different circumstances. For casual first-name greetings with neighbors, I repeat their names to myself until I'm sure I have them in mind. For family affairs, at which I will see cousins I haven't seen for a long time—and their children, whom I hardly know—I do some serious homework. That often involves making a small chart of the family, the relatives' names, and who belongs to whom. The system usually works—except for my identical twin nephews. I've spent 40 years trying to tell them apart. For a while, only one wore glasses. That helped. But when they both started wearing glasses, I was sunk.

But what did I do about the former coworker I met in the mall, whose name I could not recall? Well, that won't happen again. His name is a lot like that of a famous general, so when I meet him, I'll just think of that general, and I'll be able to come up with his name. As for trying to remember Sacramento, well, sometimes it's easier to look things up than to wait for your memory to supply the information.

• *Keeping your memory in shape.* The best way to do this, the experts say, is to keep yourself in good physical shape. Regular exercise and a proper diet will do as much good for your brain as it will for your muscles. It's also a good idea to keep your mind active, whether you play poker, chess, pool, or the stock market. Reading newspapers, magazines, or novels will help keep those brain cells humming, too.

• *Using the buddy system.* Couples or even friends can help one another remember important things. In fact, the other day, Sara suggested, "We should arrange it so that you remember all the things I forget and I'll remember all of the things you forget."

"Great idea," I said. "I'll try to remember that."

Aging and creativity

I found considerable encouragement about growing older from talking with Dr. Gene D. Cohen, director of the Center on Aging, Health and Humanities, at George Washington University in

Washington, D.C. Cohen's view is definitely upbeat. He believes that one's later years can be an extremely creative time of life—intellectually, artistically, and socially. He spells out his ideas in a book, *The Creative Age: Awakening Human Potential in the Second Half of Life*.

Cohen talked of several phases of creativity in later life. Among them are the following.

The "liberation phase"

This is a time, Cohen says, "in which creative expression is shaped by a new degree of personal freedom in retirement or the restructuring of the time commitment to family." When retirees have more free time and comfortable incomes, he relates, they often try new things, especially in the field of art. Indeed, he says, the area of folk art is dominated by older people. "For many people," Cohen says, "retirement is like a patron. A patron gives you time to do something other than having to make ends meet."

In the "liberation phase," which Cohen defines as the late fifties to early seventies, people often get a new sense of freedom to speak their minds and to do things that are courageous. Older people have played major roles in world history, Cohen notes. "The greater freedom and courage that many older adults experience," Cohen says, "help explain why a significant number of older adults about or beyond age 70 have assumed the role of 'shapers' or 'shakers' of society." Among those on Cohen's list are Socrates, Copernicus, Galileo, Mahatma Gandhi, Golda Meir, and Nelson Mandela. These movers and shakers fall into what Cohen calls social creativity with a "big C," but he talked also of social creativity with a "small c," referring to the opportunities that ordinary people have to do extraordinary things for themselves, their families, or their communities.

The summing-up phase

This is a time of life, Cohen says, "in which creative expression is shaped by the desire to find larger meaning in the story of our lives and to give in a larger way of the wisdom we have accrued."

"In the role of 'keepers of the culture,'" Cohen says, "the lessons and fortunes of a lifetime are shared through autobiography and personal storytelling, philanthropy, community activism, and volunteerism." Cohen's views should be quite encouraging to anyone approaching his or her sixties, seventies, or eighties.

Redefining old age

"The picture of late life itself has changed. It is no longer a portrait of passivity, senility, and sexlessness. Today it has become one of activity, vigor, and intellectual robustness." That quote is from Dr. Robert N. Butler, president of the International Longevity Center USA, which is affiliated with the Mount Sinai School of Medicine in New York. In a speech, Butler said he foresees a time when many people will live to 100 or beyond, will work until they are 90, and will routinely have multiple careers.

A leader in the fields of gerontology and geriatrics, Butler was the first director of the National Institute of Aging of the National Institutes of Health from 1975 to 1982. In 1976, he won a Pulitzer Prize for his book *Why Survive? Being Old in America.* "This is the first time in human history that the prospect of living a long, healthy, and productive life has become reality for the majority of people in most parts of the world. What was the privilege of the few has become the destiny of many," Butler said.

When I talked with Butler, he told me of his great interest in seeing how many older people are busy working either for pay or as volunteers, caring for grandchildren, taking part in physical-fitness programs, and traveling. This national surge of activity, Butler said, is part of "a redefinition of what later life is all about."

No doubt, this redefinition will continue. There are 35 million Americans who are over 65, and 5,000 more turn 65 each day. And the baby boomers are now coming down the road. They, too, will give retirement a new meaning.

In my senior community, for instance, I know many people whose motto is, "Eat right, exercise, and stay busy." They do. Although it is hard to see oneself as part of a historic mass movement, it's a good feeling to know that Sara and I are among the millions of people who are helping to change the meaning of old age.

The dos and don'ts of growing older

I have always believed that if something is worth doing, it is worth doing well. Golf, for instance, is much more fun when your drives are straight and your putting is accurate. If it takes a few lessons to help you get there—well, it's worth the cost. You can say the same for almost any other endeavor, including growing older. In fact, it is not hard to imagine the day when "retirement schools" may become as popular as golfing schools. Until then, learning to age gracefully will remain a do-it-yourself business.

As I grow older, and as I watch the behavior of friends and acquaintances of my age, I find myself making lists of the dos and don'ts of growing older. Together, I believe, they form a strategy that can help you age successfully and gracefully. They work for me. Hopefully, they will work for you, too.

The don'ts

- Don't bore your friends and relatives by talking on and on about your health problems. In fact, when somebody asks, "How are you?"—don't tell them.
- Don't tell the same story to the same person more than once. When you repeat your stories over and over, people think you're getting fuzzy.

- Don't neglect old friends, especially the ones who were an important part of your life. Time goes by quickly, and you don't know how many more chances you'll get to visit with those friends.

- Don't let anger rule your life. Avoid confrontation. It's an imperfect world, and people make mistakes, even when they're trying to do their best.

- Don't assume that age makes you wise and that the world is waiting for your advice. If your friends or relatives want advice, they'll ask for it.

- Don't live in the past. The past may be where you are most comfortable, but it's the present that most people—especially your children and grandchildren—really care about.

- Don't miss your opportunities. You wanted to see a baseball game last year, but you never called for tickets. You wanted to see the new art museum in town, but you never got there. Ask yourself, if you don't do those things now, when will you?

- Don't become a grumpy old man or woman. Cheerful is better. Laugh, and the world will laugh with you. Grump, and you'll grump alone.

- Don't annoy your friends and relatives with your problems. If you need a hearing aid, get a hearing aid, so that you're not always saying, "What?"

- Don't gripe about your birthdays. Enjoy them. Each year is a gift. Growing old is not a right; it's a privilege. Take a lesson from composer and pianist Eubie Blake, who lived to be 100 years old. "If I'd known I was gonna live this long," Blake said, "I'd have taken better care of myself."

The dos

- Do choose a retirement activity you really enjoy. It can be a part-time job, working as a volunteer, a hobby, or even a sport. Make that activity the focus of your life. It's wonderful to be able to spend time doing something you really like.

- Do exercise regularly. It's good for the body, but it's also good for the mind. Exercise helps reduce tension and anxiety and provides a sense of physical well-being.

- Do eat healthfully. Information on good nutrition is all around us. Figure out what foods are best for you, and include them in your daily diet. If you're confused, ask your doctor for advice.

- Do stay tuned into the world around you. It's important to stay mentally alert. Newspapers, books, magazines, and TV shows can keep you up to date on the issues of the day. Think about joining a book club. If you don't have a computer, buy one and get on the Internet.

- Do try to meet new people and develop new friendships. A good way to do that is to join a charitable, religious, or civic group. Volunteers are always welcome.

- Do maintain your physical and mental independence. For as long as your health and finances allow, try to handle your own affairs, do things for yourself, and live by your own schedule.

- Do take advantage of your experience and inner strength when personal or family troubles arise. Remember that you've spent a lifetime learning the strategies of survival. Use your knowledge to help yourself and others.

- Do pace yourself as you age. It's okay to walk a bit slower, take more time to go through the supermarket checkout line, and even drive in the slow lane. If other drivers honk at you, let them rush on by.

- Do keep your sense of humor. Make a small mental list of jokes you can tell to friends. As the *Reader's Digest* says, "Laughter is the best medicine."

• Do find a way to be friends with your children and grand-children, even though they are very busy. You need them, and whether they realize it or not, they need you.

A final word

At this point, you might say, "Now that you've told us about all those retirement decisions and dilemmas, tell us, what has retirement been like for you and Sara?" My answer may surprise you, but I am being truthful when I say, "We have had a very happy retirement."

Yes, it did take a lot of effort to get through the retirement process. And yes, I do wish I had planned my retirement with more foresight. But having said that, I can also say that the precious thing about retirement is that it has given me time: time to be creative, time to pursue personal goals, and time to see and do some of the things I didn't have time for during my 45 years of working full-time.

In addition to time, retirement has given me some important second chances: the chance to be of service to my community, the chance to explore the neglected frontiers of family and friend-ships, and, yes, the chance to slow down. It's amazing how good it feels not to be in a hurry all the time, especially when you want to simply pass the day with a relative or friend.

Finally, for Sara and me, retirement has been a special time of closeness and joy. We have led productive and exciting lives, and while we cannot predict the future, we look forward to a long and healthy retirement and wish only for the courage to make the most of whatever life brings us in the years ahead. Sara and I hope that our experiences will help you find your way to a happy retirement.

For more information

Books

Cohen, Gene, *The Creative Age: Awakening Human Potential in the Second Half of Life*, New York: Basic Books, 2006.

Cohen, Gene, *The Mature Mind. The Positive Power of the Aging Brain*, New York: Basic Books, 2006.

Hayflick, Leonard, *How and Why We Age*, New York: Ballantine Books, 1996.

Rowe, John W., and Robert L. Kahn, *Successful Aging*, New York: Pantheon Books, 1998.

Web Sites

AARP: www.aarp.org. AARP's "Internet Resources Related to Aging" (www.aarp.org/internetresources/) contains links to many other Web sites, including those related to specific diseases.

Access America for Seniors: www.seniors.gov. This is a federal interagency Web site that offers consumer information from dozens of federal and state agencies.

Administration on Aging: www.aoa.gov. Information from the federal agency that deals with issues affecting older Americans.

Elder Web: www.elderweb.com. Sources of information for professionals and family caregivers.

Elderhostel: www.elderhostel.org. Describes educational and travel programs for seniors at home and abroad.

National Institute on Aging: www.nih.gov/nia/. The latest news on federal research into aging and other age-related activities.

SeniorNet: www.seniornet.org. Founded in 1986, this organization provides computer training for older Americans at centers around the country.

Senior Sites: www.seniorsites.com. Contains a listing of nonprofit providers of senior housing, health care, and services.

Index

About the Author

Stan Hinden wrote the "Retirement Journal" column in the *Washington Post* for seven years after he retired in 1996. *How to Retire Happy* was inspired by this long-running column, which discussed the decisions, dilemmas, and challenges that confront retirees and those who are planning to retire.

The "Retirement Journal" columns were inspired in turn by the experiences, good and bad, that Stan and his wife, Sara, had as retirees. Stan's column appeared each month in the Sunday business section of the *Washington Post* from 1997 to 2004. In 1998, the *Post* nominated "Retirement Journal" for the Pulitzer Prize in Commentary. At the same time, the column won an award from the American University School of Communication and the Investment Company Institute for "excellence in personal finance reporting."

Stan has appeared on radio and television and has spoken often on the subject of "What I Wish I Had Known About Retirement." Before he retired from the *Post* in 1996, he spent 12 years writing about stocks and mutual funds in the business section. In total, he spent 23 years at the *Post* as a full-time writer and editor during his 45-year career in journalism.

Stan was born in New York City on January 27, 1927. He graduated from Syracuse University in 1950 after serving in the U.S. Army during World War II. Stan and Sara Hinden live in suburban Maryland. They have three children, four grandchildren, and one great-grandchild.